"Paul Miller has carefully observed Jesus. He has carefully observed how the work of grace unfolds in the apostle Paul's life and in his own life. Tak[e] [time] wi[th this book.] You will become a deeper, wiser, truer person. You will beco[me] [more] purposeful. And you will walk more steadily in the Light."

—[Edward Welch, Faculty member and counsel]or, [Dire]ctor of CCEF

"Never have I read a more practical work on how a Christian can flourish through deep affliction. This study will revolutionize the way you look at your sufferings and your relationship to Christ. Get ready to begin perhaps the deepest and most fulfilling Bible-adventure you've ever undertaken!"

—**Joni Eareckson Tada**,
Joni and Friends International Disability Center

"Paul Miller has a rare gift of bringing both profound encouragement and deep conviction as he throws open the curtains on the glory and grace of Jesus. *United with Christ* fills a Grand-Canyon-sized void for fresh gospel-saturated curriculum for use in our churches, small group communities, and neighborhood gatherings."

—**Scotty Smith**,
Teacher in Residence, West End Community Church (Nashville, TN)

"Nothing is more important for the gospel and for our lives as Christians than the reality of our union with Christ as Scripture teaches us about that union. Paul Miller is to be commended for seeking to apply that teaching to issues of discipleship."

—**Richard B. Gaffin, Jr.**,
Professor of Biblical and Systematic Theology, Emeritus, Westminster Theological Seminary

"These studies from Paul Miller embody everything that hungry students of God's Word should be looking for in Bible study: deep reflection on the biblical text, thoughtful bridging of the text into the reader's heart, and non-formulaic articulations of gospel truth. Eye-opening and heart-engaging."

—**Dane Ortlund**,
Executive Vice President of Bible Publishing, Crossway

"Bringing Pauline theology down to ground level, Miller's study teaches us that Paul's gospel not only calls Christians to believe in Jesus Christ but to follow him in his suffering. It is a refreshing alternative to both fluffy Bible studies and dry academics."

—**Kevin W. McFadden**,
Associate Professor of New Testament, Cairn University

J-Curve Study

UNIT 1: UNITED WITH CHRIST

Participant's Manual

Paul E. Miller

seeJesus
a global discipling mission

2018
seeJesus Press

By Paul E. Miller

The mission of seeJesus is to help people see and reflect the life, death, and resurrection of Jesus through our discipleship resources and training.

seeJesus
P.O. Box 197
Telford, PA 18969

Phone: 215.721.3113
Fax: 215.721.6535
info@seeJesus.net
www.seeJesus.net

Developmental Editor: Julie Courtney
Copyeditor and Proofreader: Lydia Leggett
Typesetter and Layout Design: Pat Reinheimer
Cover Design: Seth Guge
Inside Graphics Designer: Les Swift

© 2018 seeJesus
ISBN: 978-1-941178-21-8

DEDICATION:

In memory of Janette "Netter" O'Brien
July 11, 1972—January 13, 2015
whose love for the gospel, for the gift of free grace, was at the center of her life. We miss you!

A special thank you to:
our friends at Trinity Presbyterian Church and Christ Community Presbyterian Church
in Lakeland, Florida, and Redeemer City Church in Winter Haven, Florida—
including Keith and Payton Albritton, Mike and Janice Arnett, Howard and Deanna Bayless, Jim
and Deena Davie, Jerri and Jill Gable, David and Cynthia Hallock, Jack and Tina Harrell, Shawn
and Kelly Jones, Scott and Julie McBride, Richard Nicholson, Joe O'Brien, Dane and Tracy Parker,
Frank and Dyeanna Portlock, Sam and Victoria Portlock, Dwight and Jayna Smith, Timo and
Tina Strawbridge, Mike and Rebecca Wells, and Steve and Kinsey Young
and our friends in Pennsylvania—
including John and Pam Miller, Michael and Hyelee Yoon,
and an anonymous family foundation—
for helping make this series of six *J-Curve* studies possible.

CONTENTS

INTRODUCTION TO
THE *J-CURVE* INTERACTIVE
BIBLE STUDY SERIES

"I've believed the gospel. Now what?"

Believing *more* seems like the correct response. But the more you focus on believing, the more you struggle to live out your faith. If this describes you, you are not alone.

Scripture gives us greater guidance than "just believe." The apostle Paul explains how we live out the gospel in Philippians 3:9-10, when he aspires to:

> " [9] be found in him, not having a righteousness of my own that comes from the law, but that which comes through faith in Christ, the righteousness from God that depends on faith."

Luther's rediscovery of justification by faith—fueled by his reflection on this verse—liberated the church like never before and is rightly celebrated. But we are less enthusiastic about the truth that follows:

> " [10]— that I may know him and the power of his resurrection, and may share his sufferings, becoming like him in his death."

Paul acknowledges something we'd rather gloss over and have largely ignored as a church: Jesus' life takes a downward path into death before moving upward into resurrection.

If you think of it visually, you can trace out the letter "J." We at seeJesus call this arc of the gospel "the J-Curve." The apostle Paul describes the J-Curve as the normal Christian life[1]—a reenacting of the death and resurrection of Jesus—but it doesn't feel normal to most Christians.

The *J-Curve* Interactive Bible Study is a series of six units that search out what it means to faithfully live the kind of dying-resurrection life Paul describes in Philippians, 1 and 2 Corinthians, Philemon, and Acts.[2] By exploring these letters together, we catch Paul's radical vision of living life in the shape of the J-Curve—a vision that lies at the heart of Paul's definition of what it means to be a Christian.

Living in the *J-Curve* means we don't have to succumb to our allergy to suffering or equate God's favor with earthly success. Embracing the J-Curve renews our hope in a dark world, draws us into fellowship with God's people, and radically re-centers our daily lives on Christ. And it answers our deep and earnest question: "I've believed the gospel. Now what?"

---

[1] Phil. 1:29, 2:5-9, 3:10-11

[2] The theme is dominant in these Pauline letters but muted somewhat in Romans and Galatians.

Unit 1: United With Christ

Union with Christ—being "in Christ"—doesn't sound like the solution to a real problem. But a careful study of Philippians 3:1-11 reveals that our problems with legalism and the Flesh are solved by our union with Christ. Justification by faith liberates us from human pride and despair by giving us righteousness as a gift. This lays the groundwork for understanding how the J-Curve builds on justification by faith and makes union with Christ come alive in a way that simply believing the gospel by itself doesn't.

Unit 2: The Descent of Love

We take a closer look at the patterns and structure of the J-Curve through this study of Philippians 2:1-9, discovering how humility and incarnation shape the downward journey into death. Understanding that our justification is grounded in Jesus' resurrection, we see that the J-Curve is the shape of both unity and purity in the church. We then explore how the J-Curve looks in Paul's life and in the lives of his fellow workers and how he calls the Philippians to live it out.

Unit 3: The Wisdom of the Cross

The Corinthian church is familiar with justification by faith, but the gospel sits like a mist over their essentially pagan ways of relating to one another. So Paul doesn't just preach the gospel to these believers. He embodies it, living out the J-Curve among them as one who is "enslaved by the gospel." As we study 1 Corinthians, we begin to see how the J-Curve shapes the way a gospel community lives together.

Unit 4: Thorn in the Flesh

In 2 Corinthians—Paul's "Romans" for the J-Curve—Paul digs deeper into the J-Curve life when he is attacked by the Corinthian church. His pattern of not just believing the gospel but also reenacting it produces a gospel community that reflects the dying-resurrection life of Jesus and leads to Paul's reconciliation with the church.

Unit 5: Transformed by Hope

We follow Paul in Acts as he journeys to Jerusalem and then Rome, watching how he experiences the dying and rising of Jesus in the midst of beatings, imprisonments, and persecution of all types. His everyday experience of suffering is transformed by the hope he has in Christ, and that transformation impacts the shape of his gospel community. The book of Philemon provides a glimpse into what that community looked like for Paul.

Unit 6: Immersed in Gospel Community

We begin with the Gospels, looking at how Jesus lays the groundwork for a distinctive gospel community and then how Paul carries that out in his Greco-Roman context. This final J-Curve study gives us a vision for this type of gospel-shaped community—balancing the outward forces of mission with the inward forces of community—where Jesus' death and resurrection is continually reenacted. Spoiler alert: it is a touch of heaven!

KEY CONCEPTS OF
J-CURVE STUDY,
UNIT 1: UNITED WITH CHRIST

The gospel isn't for just the beginning of the Christian life, but the whole life.

1. Our Flesh is allergic to God, the true source of life, and is always seeking alternative sources of life. It wants to be "in" something other than God.
2. Legalism is the Flesh's measuring rod. If I'm not that bad, then following a few rules is all I need.
3. Union with Christ isn't just a theological idea. We are always in union with something, either an idol or God. We naturally want "in."
4. Union with Christ is the frame for justification by faith. Justification by faith is inseparable from being "in Jesus."
5. Justification is wholly a work of God received by faith. Even faith is a gift of the Spirit.
6. Justification by faith shapes how we do life. It frees us from both the pursuit of boasting and also the fear of failure and draws us into Christ.
7. The J-Curve describes Jesus' path downward into death and upward into resurrection.
8. The normal Christian life looks like the J-Curve. We are always dying and rising.
9. We don't just believe the gospel; we become like the gospel in our lives. We reenact his dying and rising.
10. The "fellowship of his sufferings . . . and power of his resurrection" (the J-Curve) provides a missing grounding for love.

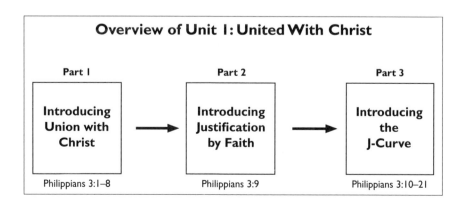

SIMPLIFIED GLOSSARY
OF TERMS

(Definitions are in approximate order of their appearance in the manual.)

PART 1: Union with Christ

Flesh: Paul the apostle uses "the Flesh" in several distinct ways. Most frequently, he uses "Flesh" to describe our sinful nature, our natural bent towards evil which causes us to obsess over ourselves and rebel against God. These two aspects of the Flesh are connected: because we are allergic to God (we don't want anyone telling us what to do), we are self-absorbed. We reverse the two great commandments. Instead of loving others, we love ourselves; instead of loving God, we love other gods. Our Flesh, at its core, is our determination to seek a source of life other than God. We believe that we can do life by our own power and effort. (We capitalize "Flesh" when the apostle Paul uses it to describe our sinful nature.)

Idolatry: Alternative sources of life, other gods to worship. Because of our Flesh's dislike of God, we are always looking for other gods to worship. We can turn almost anything in creation into an idol—sports, children, marriage, or work. We are, as John Calvin said, a "perpetual factory of idols."

Self-righteousness: Self-righteousness is the "shine" or "glow" of the Flesh. It's our belief in our own goodness which leads to our quickness to proclaim our goodness and to defend against criticism. Because the Flesh is evil, it constantly declares its goodness. Evil always masks itself as goodness.

Boasting: Because we are self-righteous, we boast. Boasting is simply going public with our view of ourselves. Left to our own devices, we subtly but relentlessly market ourselves.

Legalism: The law is good; in fact, it gives us a wise path to follow. But because of the Flesh's confident self-righteousness, we believe that we can both please ourselves and God by merely doing the right thing on our own. Then rules or "keeping the law" become a yardstick that show us (as well as God and others) how good we are. In other words, our Flesh corrupts the law. We lose sight of the heart of the law—love for God and neighbor—and put rules ahead of people.

Judaizers: Some Jewish Christians demanded that Gentile Christians must follow the Jewish law, especially circumcision. Like all legalists, Judaizers underestimated the power of the Flesh.

Union with Christ: We are all in union with something. If you get married, you are both "in" one another. If you idolize something, you are "in" it. Likewise, as Christians, we are "in" Jesus and he is "in" us. We are even "in Jesus" in his death and resurrection.

PART 2: Justification by Faith

Justification by Faith: Because of Jesus' death on the cross for us, the Father counts us righteous. Because of Jesus' obedience to death for us, we are forgiven for our sins and declared righteous. Because we are "in Christ," all that Christ has becomes ours.

Faith: Faith looks away from self to Jesus. Because this is impossible for the Flesh, even faith must be a gift from God. Faith does not save us, but it connects us to Jesus who can. Because faith despairs of self, it has nothing to boast about. Faith surrenders the boast.

Sanctification: The lifelong process of becoming like Jesus.

PART 3: The J-Curve

Gospel: Gospel means "good news." It is the story of Jesus' life, death, and resurrection for our sins, breaking both the guilt and the power of our sin.

J-Curve: The gospel is shaped like the letter "J." Jesus goes downward from life into death and then upward into resurrection. The J-Curve (the story of Jesus' life, death, and resurrection) is the pattern for the normal Christian life. We are continually drawn down into death and up into resurrection by our love and witness. We are always dying and rising. The J-Curve is the DNA of the Christian life.

Believing and Becoming Like the Gospel: The foundation of the Christian life is believing the gospel, resting in Jesus' work. But we also become like the gospel. That is, Jesus' humility and obedience leading to his death defines for us a life of others-centered love. So we not only believe the gospel, we also become like the gospel.

Already, Not Yet: Between Jesus' resurrection and his return, we live in an unusual, in-between time. For example, because of Jesus' death and resurrection for us, we are *already* forgiven and counted righteous, but we still struggle with the Flesh. So we are *not yet* righteous in all our thoughts and actions. *Already* we experience Jesus' resurrection by his Spirit who lives in us, but our bodies have *not yet* experienced that resurrection.

PART 1:
UNION WITH CHRIST

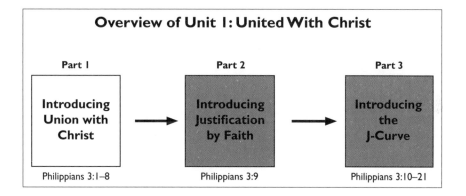

Overview of Unit 1: United With Christ

Part 1		Part 2		Part 3
Introducing Union with Christ	→	**Introducing Justification by Faith**	→	**Introducing the J-Curve**
Philippians 3:1–8		Philippians 3:9		Philippians 3:10–21

LESSON 1: IN THE FLESH

SECTION 1: The Legalist's Boast

Philippians 3:1-6

> [1] Finally, my brothers, rejoice in the Lord. To write the same things to you is no trouble to me and is safe for you. [2] Look out for the dogs, look out for the evildoers, look out for those who mutilate the flesh. [3] For we are the circumcision, who worship by the Spirit of God and *boast*[1] in Christ Jesus and put no confidence in the flesh—[4] though I myself have reason for confidence in the flesh also. If anyone else thinks he has reason for confidence in the flesh, I have more: [5] circumcised on the eighth day, of the people of Israel, of the tribe of Benjamin, a Hebrew of Hebrews; as to the law, a Pharisee; [6] as to zeal, a persecutor of the church; as to righteousness under the law, blameless.

Historical Background: Judaizers

The people Paul warns about were called Judaizers. They were Jewish Christian missionaries, not approved by the Jerusalem Church, who wanted Gentile Christians to become Jews in practice by being circumcised.[2] In their view, Gentiles had to keep the law in order to be truly part of the people of God (see Gen. 17). Judaizers said that "Jesus + law obedience = salvation."[3]

1. What do you think Paul is referring to when he says these people "mutilate the flesh"?

---

[1] I've changed the ESV *glory* to *boast* because it is a more literal translation, and *boasting* is a major theme in Paul that gets lost because the Greek work is translated as either *boast (NIV)*, *glory (ESV)* or *rejoice*. See Thielman, *The NIV Application Commentary: Philippians*, 168.

[2] Summary by Dr. Kevin McFadden, personal note to the author.

[3] For a full explanation, see Tom Schreiner, *Circumcision* in Hawthorne, Dictionary of Paul and His Letters.

Historical Background: Legalism

- Paul didn't care if someone was circumcised or uncircumcised (Gal. 6:15; 1 Cor. 7:19). He even circumcised Timothy so as to not offend Jewish believers since Timothy's mother was Jewish (Acts 16:3). What Paul was opposed to was circumcision as a requirement for justification or salvation (Gal. 5:2-4).[4]
- 1st century Judaism, like all legalism, was concerned for formal, outward purity that forgot about people.
- In legalism, the outer ritual and performance is all-important as opposed to inward change and deeper issues of the heart.

Entrance to a mikveh filled with water south of the Temple Mount in Jerusalem.[5]

2. As you look at this historical background, what are some of the patterns of the Judaizers' approach to "goodness"?

[4]   Summary by Dr. Kevin McFadden.

[5]   Photo courtesy of Todd Bolen/BiblePlaces.com

3. How is reliance on ourselves a very modern solution to our problems?

4. We look back on mikvehs and say "how odd," but what modern efforts do we make at self-improvement? What do we obsess over?

Summary of Observations on Legalism:
1. Legalism focuses on outward behavior and not the heart.
2. Legalism focuses on appearance, on outward purity instead of inward purity.
3. The legalist doesn't think he is that bad, so he is confident he can change himself.

Definition of Legalism: The law is good; in fact, it gives us a wise path to follow. But because of the Flesh's confident self-righteousness, we believe that we can both please ourselves and God by merely doing the right thing on our own. Then rules or "keeping the law" become a yardstick that show us (as well as God and others) how good we are. In other words, our Flesh corrupts the law. We lose sight of the heart of the law—love for God and neighbor—and put rules ahead of people.

SECTION 2: Paul's Reaction to Boasting

5. What three things does Paul call the Judaizers in verse 2?

 Literary Background: Paul's Warning
Each of the three words (dogs, evil, mutilate) begins with the "k" sound, adding to the punch. This is called alliteration. A translation closer to the feel of the Greek (3:2) reads:

Look out for those *dogs*! *kunas*

Look out for *evil workers*! *kakous*

Look out for the *mutilation*! *katatomen*

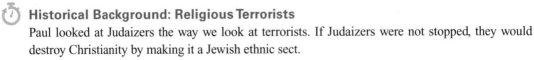

Historical Background: Religious Terrorists

Paul looked at Judaizers the way we look at terrorists. If Judaizers were not stopped, they would destroy Christianity by making it a Jewish ethnic sect.

Literary Background: Paul's Warning

With each of the three names, Paul subtly calls the Judaizers pagans—the very people they despised.

1st: "Dogs" was a religious term.

2nd: "Evil workers."

3rd: "The mutilation" is a pun.

SECTION 3: Paul the Apostle's Boast

6. Read 3:3. Who is the "we" in 3:3? How does this reverse what the Judaizers thought?

🕐 **Theological Background: Circumcision of the Heart**

The Old Testament (Deut. 10:16, Jer. 4:4) tells us that Israel needs circumcision of the heart.

📄 **Literary Background: "Boast in Christ Jesus"** [6]

"Boast in Christ Jesus and put no confidence in the flesh" is written in an X-pattern.[7] Similar letters (A and A') indicate similar ideas.

A Boasting
B in Christ Jesus
B' and not in the Flesh
A' Putting confidence

7. **"Boasting in _____" and "confidence in _____" serve the same purpose. What does boasting or confidence in something do for us?**

8. **Let's list what Paul's Flesh is confident in before he met Jesus.**

   1.

   2.

   3.

---

[6] The Greek word *boast* has a broader meaning than the more negative English word so it is translated as either *boast* (NIV), *glory* (ESV), or rejoice. I've used *boast* because it is a major theme in Paul's writings that can get lost. See Thielman, *Philippians*, 168, and Silva, *Philippians*, 147.

[7] O'Brien, *Philippians*, 363.

4.

5.

6.

7.

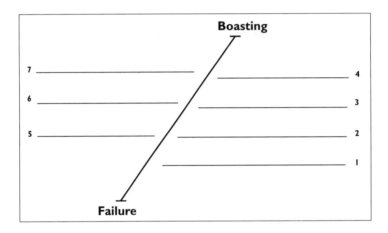

9. Let's construct our own chart similar to the apostle Paul's. Think of a personal boast you've either said or thought. I'll write them down.

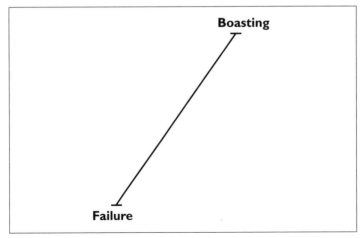

Unit 1: United With Christ

In a shame-honor culture (which was all of the ancient world) your primary identity is given at birth. So the first four items belonged to Paul as the son of well-born Jewish parents. Paul was upper-class Judaism.

10. How do we see legalism in Paul's list of virtues? What is legalism focused on?

SECTION 4: The Flesh

11. When Paul says "Flesh" in 3:3-4, what do you think he means?

Definition of the Flesh

Paul the apostle uses "the Flesh" in several distinct ways.

12. Why does the Flesh like legalism?

13. Why doesn't legalism work?

14. What is the relationship between legalism and "the Flesh"?

LESSON 1 APPLICATION

Reflecting on Legalism

1. Legalism makes the rule more important than people. Can you think of an example where you've seen legalism, where someone has a personal rule that forgets about people?

2. Can you think of an example in your life where you've had a personal rule that forgets about people?

3. What are forms of legalism in our modern culture—either secular or Christian?

4. Why are we so quick to become legalists?

Reflect on the Failure-Boasting Chart

Construct your own Failure-Boasting Chart based on your personal boasts, either current ones or those that you've had in the past.

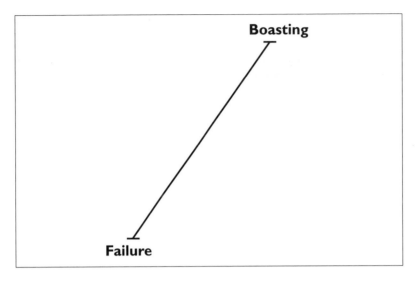

Reflect on the Flesh

5. Based on this lesson, create your own personalized definition of the Flesh using the word "me." Share these with the group.

6. Can you think of one area of your life that might be an "alternative source of life"?

7. Using your answer above, make a list, similar to Paul the apostle's list, which shows how you either feel or boast about this.

8. Read Mark 7:1-23. What similarities do you see between what Jesus says and what Paul says?

9. What is one insight you've had from your study today that you'd like to hang onto in the week to come?

LESSON 2: MARKETING THE SELF

Philippians 3:3-9

[3] For we are "the circumcision," who worship by the Spirit of God and *boast* in Christ Jesus and not in the flesh putting confidence—[4] though I myself have reason for confidence in the flesh also. If anyone else thinks he has reason for confidence in the flesh, I have more:

[5] circumcised on the eighth day,
of the people of Israel,
of the tribe of Benjamin,
a Hebrew of Hebrews;
as to the law, a Pharisee;
[6] as to zeal, a persecutor of the church;
as to righteousness under the law, blameless.

[7] But whatever gain I had, I counted as loss for the sake of Christ.[8] Indeed, I count everything as loss because of the surpassing worth of knowing Christ Jesus my Lord. For his sake I have suffered the loss of all things and count them as rubbish, in order that I may gain Christ [9] and be found in him, not having a righteousness of my own that comes from the law, but that which comes through faith in Christ, the righteousness from God that depends on faith.

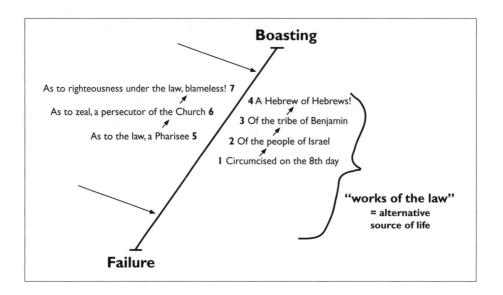

Boasting

As to righteousness under the law, blameless! **7**

As to zeal, a persecutor of the Church **6**

As to the law, a Pharisee **5**

4 A Hebrew of Hebrews!

3 Of the tribe of Benjamin

2 Of the people of Israel

1 Circumcised on the 8th day

"works of the law"
= alternative
source of life

Failure

1. You can feel Paul's emotions as he rehearses these two lists. What is the emotional dynamic or direction for each of the lists?

2. Why does Paul build each list to a climax? What does that reflect?

3. **What is Paul doing with the Judaizers' confidence in the Flesh? Read 3:4b.**

🕐 **Historical Background: "Works of the Law"**
In Romans and Galatians, Paul's phrase for this list of seven items is "works of the law." The only other place the phrase is used in Paul's day is a Dead Sea Scroll from Qumran, a strict Jewish sect that lived near the Dead Sea.[1]

SECTION 2: Boasting—A Universal Problem

4. **In 3:9, what phrase does Paul use to describe this list?**

5. **Since this is a "Jewish" list, why doesn't Paul say "confidence in being a faithful *Jew*"? Why does Paul say "confidence in the *Flesh*"? What's the difference?**

🕐 **Theological Background: Self-Righteousness—A Universal Problem[2]**
Paul moves from the narrow world of Jewish identity to the broader world of the human heart with the phrase "confidence in the Flesh." All humanity tries to root itself in something other than God; we are universally tempted to have something outside of ourselves that forms the basis of who we are. If the problem of "confidence in the Flesh" is universal, then the solution—Jesus—must be universal.

Envy.

---

[1] See Appendix: Lesson Note 4.

[2] See Appendix: Lesson Note 3, for more background on this question.

Boasting.

Judging.

Gossip.

Divisions.

Narcissism.

Materialism.

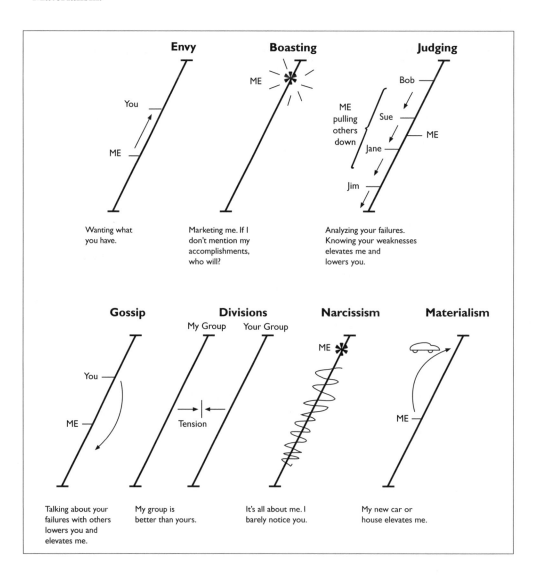

Envy — Wanting what you have.

Boasting — Marketing me. If I don't mention my accomplishments, who will?

Judging — Analyzing your failures. Knowing your weaknesses elevates me and lowers you.

Gossip — Talking about your failures with others lowers you and elevates me.

Divisions — My group is better than yours.

Narcissism — It's all about me. I barely notice you.

Materialism — My new car or house elevates me.

Personal Illustration: Not Boasting

Many years ago towards the end of an hour-long meeting with my boss and our communications director, I realized that it was not clear that I was the one who had the idea we had been talking about. At least no one had mentioned my role in coming up with this idea. Their vision seemed dim. I began to think how I could remedy this oversight by saying something like, "When I first came up with this idea . . . ." The question to myself was, "How can I get the credit due me without appearing proud?" I wasn't going to directly boast, but I wanted to give them some background so they were aware of my role.

But I'd been reading John 6 about feeding on Jesus, so I was silent. I knew I would be feeding on their praise of me by boasting. When the meeting ended, I felt an overwhelming sense of despair and loneliness, like there was no point to life anymore. I was surprised by the strength of that feeling.

When the room emptied out, I turned off the lights and went over to the window. I was overcome with an enormous hunger for Christ. I'd been reading and meditating on John 6, where Jesus, by the seaside at Capernaum, encounters the crowd the morning after he had fed them. So I opened to John 6 and read:

> **51** "I am the living bread that came down from heaven. If anyone eats of this bread, he will live forever. And the bread that I will give for the life of the world is my flesh . . . ." **55** For my flesh is true food, and my blood is true drink. **56** Whoever feeds on my flesh and drinks my blood abides in me, and I in him. **57** As the living Father sent me, and I live because of the Father, so whoever feeds on me, he also will live because of me."

6. In Paul Miller's mind, where was he located on the Failure-Boasting chart?

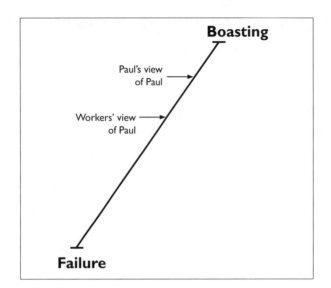

7. Read vs. 3:9. What was Paul Miller trying to create by boasting?

8. Why were Paul Miller's feelings so powerful when he didn't boast? Why did he feel so empty?

9. What happened after Paul Miller felt so empty?

Gospel Connection: Faith Replaces Marketing the Self
Paul Miller moved from wanting his co-workers to "see Paul" to wanting to "see Jesus" himself. The same shift happens in Philippians 3:5-9.

LESSON 2 APPLICATION

Reflect on Paul Miller's Desire to Boast

1. Can you recall an experience where you felt the emptiness of your Flesh?

2. Can you think of ways that you, like the apostle Paul, draw your identity from things that were given to you? (Family background, family accomplishments, schooling, family finances, your country, your country's accomplishments, etc.)

3. What is one insight you've had from your study today that you'd like to hang onto in the week to come?

Boasting Log. Just for this week, keep a record of every time you boast or have a boastful thought. This might include judgmental comments you make to yourself about how other people drive, their weight, appearance, or attitude. For example, you see an overweight person and think something like, "She's fat . . . I would never look like that . . . she eats too much." These thoughts come so fast that we aren't even aware that we are thinking them. Note also how you respond to either criticism or the threat of criticism. Write down the date, location, and a half sentence summary of your boast. A sample is below. The actual log is on the second page. Personally, I (Paul Miller) have done this and been amazed at how much I either boast or have boastful thoughts. The opposite of this is people who always see themselves as failures.

DATE	LOCATION	MY THOUGHTS OR ACTIONS	REFLECTIONS ON MY BOASTING
June 2	At the mall	Saw overweight woman. Thought she ate too much.	I was superior to this woman.
	On the phone with a friend.	Talked about a woman at church who irritates me. My friend agreed with me.	My friend and I formed a little community who understood how difficult this woman was. It felt good to have someone understand me. But I've avoided the painful community that would come from talking to this woman face to face. Even though she thinks she is above us, our conversation made us feel we were above her.

Boasting Log for _____

DATE	LOCATION	MY THOUGHTS OR ACTIONS	REFLECTIONS ON MY BOASTING

DATE	LOCATION	MY THOUGHTS OR ACTIONS	REFLECTIONS ON MY BOASTING

LESSON 3: IN JESUS

SECTION 1: In Him

Philippians 3:7-9

> [7] But whatever gain I had, I counted as loss for the sake of Christ. [8] Indeed, I count everything as loss because of the surpassing worth of knowing Christ Jesus my Lord. For his sake I have suffered the loss of all things and count them as rubbish, in order that I may gain Christ [9] and be found in him, not having a righteousness of my own that comes from the law, but that which comes through faith in Christ, the righteousness from God that depends on faith—

1. Specifically, in verse 9, where does Paul want to be?

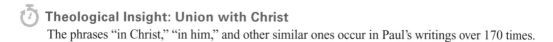

Theological Insight: Union with Christ
The phrases "in Christ," "in him," and other similar ones occur in Paul's writings over 170 times.

2. So before Paul was a Christian, where was he "located"? What was his life source? If you had to pick one word, what was Paul "in"?

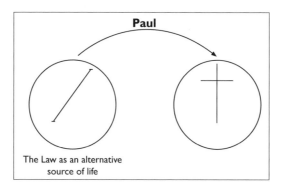

Paul

The Law as an alternative
source of life

3. **What's the problem with saying you are "in Jesus"? How does it feel if I say, "Good news, you are 'in Jesus'"?**

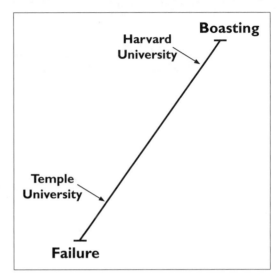

 Personal Illustration: In Harvard

When I was in high school, my oldest sister went to Wellesley College and introduced me to the world of Ivy League schools. She said, "Paul, you could get into Harvard." Getting into Harvard would identify me as one of the elite of our culture. That, in turn, would open all kinds of doors. I wanted to be "in Harvard." Of course, I didn't get in. Nor did I get into Yale or Princeton. Instead I went to Temple University.

I have a humble friend who did go to Harvard. When he talks about something that happened at Harvard, he'll say, "When I was at college." The first time I heard him say "college," I wondered why he didn't say, "Harvard." On the other hand, I usually say "college" because Temple doesn't give me much of an identity! A couple of times I've found myself quoting my friend saying, "My friend, who went to Harvard . . ."! By linking myself to my friend, I elevate the value of my comment and create a virtual link to Harvard. My friend who went to Harvard doesn't mention Harvard because he is "in Jesus." But I, who didn't go to Harvard, 40 years later am still trying to get "in Harvard." God be merciful to me, a sinner!

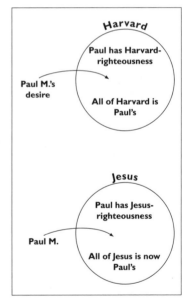

4. In 3:9 Paul talks about "a righteousness of my own that comes from the law." How would you paraphrase that for Paul Miller's desire to go to Harvard?

Comparison Chart: In Harvard vs. In Jesus

	IN HARVARD	IN JESUS
How do you get in?		
Whose record is on the application?		
What group lets you "in"?		
Who gets in?		
Formal ceremony for admissions?		
How do you participate?		

(Chart continued on the next page)

	IN HARVARD	IN JESUS
Whom do you meet?		
What symbols do you wear?		
What do you get when you leave?		
What happens if you destroy Harvard or Jesus physically?		
What happens if you destroy society's esteem of Harvard and Jesus?		

SECTION 3: The Inner Ring

Alan Jacobs discusses the Inner Ring using a speech by C. S. Lewis.

> In December 1944, C. S. Lewis speaking to his Oxford students said "in every human institution" is a "second or unwritten system" that stands next to the formal organization.
> "You discover gradually, in almost indefinable ways, that it exists and that you are outside it. . . . It is not easy, even at a given moment, to say who is inside and who is outside. . . . People think they are in it after they have in fact been pushed out of it, or before they have been allowed in; this provides great amusement for those who are really inside."

     Unit 1: United With Christ

"I believe that in all men's lives . . . one of the most dominant elements is the desire to be inside the local Ring and the terror of being left outside . . . Unless you take measures to prevent it, this desire is going to be one of the chief motives of your life, from the first day on which you enter your profession until the day when you are too old to care."

". . . Of all passions, the passion for the Inner Ring is most skillful in making a man, who is not yet a very bad man, do very bad things."

The draw of the Inner Ring has such profound, corrupting power because it never announces itself as evil. Lewis goes on, ". . . The choice which could lead to scoundrelism will come . . . . Over a drink or a cup of coffee, disguised as a triviality and sandwiched between two jokes . . . the hint will come . . . you will be drawn in, if you are drawn in, not by desire for gain or ease, but simply because at that moment, when the cup was so near your lips, you cannot bear to be thrust back again into the cold outer world."

What many young people want, and especially the intellectuals and artists, is . . . "the sacred little attic or studio, the heads bent together . . . and the delicious knowledge that we—we four or five all huddled beside this stove—are the people who know. In short what the Inner Ring. . . offers is precisely what the serpent offered Eve . . . the knowledge that makes mere people into Gods. 'Your genuine Inner Ring exists for exclusion.'"[1]

5. How does a dirty joke create an invitation to be part of an inner ring? What happens if you don't laugh?

6. How is gossip a way of getting into an inner ring? What happens if you don't participate in gossip?

---

[1] C. S. Lewis, December 1944, Commemoration Oration at King's College, London, quoted in Jacobs, *The Narnian*, 178-180.

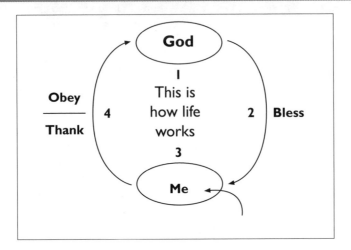

All of Life Is Gift

This is the basic structure of the universe. This isn't only how God relates to us, but also how we relate to one another.

7. Of these four elements in this chart, which one failed; which one is the weak link?

8. What is the root problem with in-the-law Paul *and* us?

Romans 8:3

"For God has done what the law, *weakened by the flesh*, could not do. By sending his own Son in the likeness of sinful flesh and for sin, he condemned sin in the flesh . . . ."

9. **How did pre-Christian Paul use the law? What did the law do for him?**

⊚ Gospel Connection: The Law Is Not Defective

We live in a moral universe that reflects the character of God. The law is not defective. The problem is with the human heart. God's solution to the problem of our hearts was putting his Son in our place.

10. **According to Galatians, what can't the law do?**

LESSON 3 APPLICATION

Reflect on Your Boasting Log

1. How did you do on your "boasting log"? What were some of your observations about yourself?

Reflect on "In Harvard"

2. What are the "Harvards" to which you are drawn? Are there idols in your life?

Reflect on Your "Inner Ring"

3. Have you seen anyone being drawn into the combination of unbelief and sexual impurity through the power of the "inner ring"? Describe.

4. How would you prepare someone younger not to be drawn into the seduction of being "on the inside"?

5. Which "inner rings" tempt you? How do you get "in"? What do you have to do, say, or look like to be accepted into an inner ring?

6. Reflecting on the seductive power of the inner ring, recall a time when you felt seduced by its pull. What happened?

7. How might being "in Jesus" keep you from being drawn into an inner ring?

8. How can you cultivate being "in Jesus" this week? What can you do to guard yourself from being drawn into an inner ring?

All of Life Is Gift

Reading: "Everything Is a Gift from God" by Peter Kreeft[2]

Everything is a gift. Nature, people, things, events—all the things in our lives that we take for granted—are granted to us and given to us actively and deliberately by God the giver.

This gives us a whole new way of looking at things. We usually see them as only *things*. But they are *signs*. A sign is not only a thing, but it also has another level of meaning. For instance, a road sign on a metal post along the roadway is first of all a thing, but it is also a sign. As a thing, it is simply a flat metal surface with a painted design of some sort placed along the roadway. But as a sign, it means something else. It means what it points to. For instance, it might tell us New York City is forty miles away in a certain direction.

When we give a gift, it is not only a thing but also a sign of something: a sign of our love perhaps. We want the recipient of the gift not only to get a thing—like candy or flowers—but also "to get the message." We communicate that we care about them enough to give them a gift.

All the things in this world are gifts and signs. As gifts, they point beyond themselves to the divine giver. As signs, they point beyond themselves to the God they signify and reveal, as a letter reveals the writer. And since God is love, the one thing everything signifies is God's love to us. The whole world is a love letter from God.

Bernard of Clairvaux, a Doctor of the Church and a great lover of God, said that when he looked at

---

[2] After writing that "all of life is gift" (section 4 of this lesson), I discovered that Peter Kreeft had written the same thing. See #4 in the blog entry, "The Twelve Most Profound Ideas I Ever Had," www.peterkreeft.com/topics-more/12-ideas.htm.

a crucifix, the wounds of Christ seemed like lips speaking to him and saying, "I love you." Everything is like that. Everything is God's lips speaking love, God's message to us. Everything has its meaning here between God and us, not in itself. Everything is relative to this absolute.

This way of looking at things, as gifts and signs rather than simply as things in themselves, is not our usual way of seeing. Try this new way for just one hour and see the difference it makes. See the sunrise not as a mindless, mechanical necessity but as God's smile. See a wave not just as tons of cold salt water crashing down on the shore but as God's playful action. See even death as not just a biological necessity but as God tucking us in at bedtime so that we can rise to new life in the morning.

This is not a trick we play on ourselves or a fantasy. This is what the world really is. It is just as true to say that every snowflake is a gift of God, as it is true to say that every cent in a father's inheritance is a gift to his children. It is just as true to say that every leaf on every tree is a work of art made by the divine artist with the intention that we see it, know it, love it, and rejoice in it, as it is true to say that every word in a lover's letter to his beloved is meant to be seen, known, loved, and enjoyed. This is not fantasy. What is fantasy, is the horrible habit the modern world has gotten itself into, the habit of thinking that what the world really is, is only atoms and chance, only what the senses and science reveal, the view that everything else is mere subjective fancy.

9. What strikes or convicts you about Peter Kreeft's insights?

10. How is it different from how we normally think or see?

11. What is one insight you've had from your study today that you'd like to hang onto in the week to come?

12. Begin each morning this week by thanking God for the gifts of the previous day. Be prepared to share this next week when you get together again.

LESSON 4: IN MINISTRY

Philippians 3:3-9

[3] For we are "the circumcision," who worship by the Spirit of God and *boast* in Christ Jesus and not in the flesh putting confidence—[4] though I myself have reason for confidence in the flesh also. If anyone else thinks he has reason for confidence in the flesh, I have more:

> [5] circumcised on the eighth day,
>> of the people of Israel,
>>> of the tribe of Benjamin,
>>>> a Hebrew of Hebrews;
> as to the law, a Pharisee;
>> [6] as to zeal, a persecutor of the church;
>>> as to righteousness under the law, blameless.

[7] But whatever gain I had, I counted as loss for the sake of Christ. [8] Indeed, I count everything as loss because of the surpassing worth of knowing Christ Jesus my Lord. For his sake I have suffered the loss of all things and count them as rubbish, in order that I may gain Christ [9] and be found in him, not having a righteousness of my own that comes from the law, but that which comes through faith in Christ, the righteousness from God that depends on faith.

1. **According to the old Paul, what does God think of him and all his wonderful virtues? What is he attempting to do before God with his list of seven successes?**

2. So what was "old" Paul doing with the law in relationship to God? What does his obedience to the law do for him?[1]

3. What is the irony of the law being Paul's "alternative source of life"?

Jesus Insight: Dependence

Paul is boasting, using the law to be *independent* of God.[2] Jesus, on the other hand, is dependent on his Father. "I do nothing on my own; I do just what I see my Father doing" (John 5:19). He shared our flesh in that he was a human being, but he did not share in the sin of our flesh. In this sense, Jesus has no Flesh, no "alternative source of life," only his Father.[3]

SECTION 2: A Wife's Letter

Dear Tim,   April, 1983

I deeply appreciate the honesty and integrity of your life as you stand before God. You have a willingness to listen and to obey as evidenced by your submission to him during these past weeks. Many difficulties and problems were met and dealt with. As we read David Mains'

---

[1] This is an inference from the whole of Paul's thought. Paul never uses this specific language. But Paul's explanations of how the law functioned in his pre-Christian life (Phil. 3:4-6, Gal. 1) all point to the law as a source of life. It was Paul's boast. In that sense, it was antithetical to his new boast in Christ. Therefore, it functions exactly as an idol would. Paul repeatedly says that the law doesn't give life. This is not the only way that the law functions in Paul's thinking. He always affirms the goodness of the law. See Thielman, *Paul and the Law*.

[2] Tannehill, *Dying and Rising with Christ*, 124.

[3] Kevin McFadden (PhD), personal communication with author: "Paul is careful to show his readers that Jesus was fully human and yet did not partake in our sin. Paul says Jesus was born in the line of David 'according to the flesh' (Rom. 1:3), but he distances Jesus from our sin by saying he was sent 'in the *likeness* of sinful flesh'" (Rom. 8:3). See also Moo, *Romans*, 479–480.

article together and discussed his failures in the light of your ministry, I again saw you learn from him and apply his insights into your own life and ministry. This gives me much confidence as I write this letter to you that together we can learn from one another.

When Karen Mains wrote about her husband having a mistress (Circle Church) in Chicago, we both laughed, and my response was that you had two mistresses—our church and our work in Africa. We laughed together.

As I write this letter, I am aware that many of the things that concern me, you are already repenting for, but my concern for both of us is that our repentance together go deeper. As I watch you in your struggles and labors and your desire to be God's man in this 20th century, I also see the mission work and the church taking your time and energies. They are the source of your deepest joys and greatest fears. You nourish and cherish them as a bridegroom his bride. When we wake up in the morning your thoughts are usually on the church, the discipleship group, neighbors, … your writing, the missions team, and your teaching and preaching.

Your daytime energies are directed in these areas, and at night, they are still with you. I don't mean to imply that this is all in the energy of the Flesh. No one could do all these things unless empowered by the Holy Spirit. I am saying that, as I study Ephesians 5, I read that there is a holy energy that goes into marriage from the husband to the wife.

The other day when I asked if we could have tea together or just go out, I wanted to say some of these things, but your response was: "I thought we had enough of problems." I forgive you, and I forgive you for making the church and the mission your first love, but I'm not sure I am helping you by keeping quiet.

Tim, I am loyal to you. I have followed you all over the world. I will even die for you. However, when we were in the airport before coming home, you started to talk about your concerns about our relationship. I said at the time that I am often left to figure out before God what my problems are, and, in the process, I become detached and independent.

I have learned to accept this as a way of life, but is it God's norm? You often say you want to be a man controlled and compelled by the promises of Scripture, a man of prayer and patience, and a perpetual learner. God is making you all of this, but I rarely hear you desire to be taught how to nourish and cherish your wife as Christ does the church.

I trust we are past the thinking, "If I change she will change," or "If he changes I will change," but I believe before God we need change: I, in heart submission to you as a man and my husband and not just my pastor or teacher, and you in the area of nourishing and cherishing.

I am not sure at this point where to begin. Maybe we can ask an elder to pray for us. I have often thought that I lost a husband when you took your first pastorate, and I'm not sure I have ever gotten him back.

I used to feel incredibly guilty in my relationship to you and my often lack of affectionate response. I am still left with the feeling that there used to be more than this. However, I am confident that he who has begun a good work in us will continue it until the day of Christ. Thank you for listening.
Love, Janet

4. What strikes you about this letter?

5. According to Janet, what is Tim "in"? What was his "alternative source of life"?

Ⓣ **Historical Background: Augustine on Love**

The Church Father, Augustine of Hippo, described our fallen nature as having "disordered love." That is, our loves are out of order. God should be first and ministry second. When that order is reversed, our loves are mixed up or disordered.

6. How does Tim being *in ministry* affect his relationship with Janet? Be specific.

7. Why do idols (alternative sources of life) mess up our relationships?

8. What biblical word describes what Janet is putting her finger on in Tim's life?

9. Why is it particularly hard to see "In Ministry" as an alternative source of life?

10. **How is Tim's "In Ministry" similar to Paul the apostle's being "In the Law" (his list of seven boasts)?**

11. **Think of Paul's phrase, "a righteousness of my own that comes from the law." How does that apply to Tim? What is Tim doing?**

12. **Tim believed and preached "a righteousness from God that depends on faith." So what is Tim missing?**

13 **If Tim were to rest in a righteousness "which comes through faith in Christ," how would that change him? How would it change how he relates to Janet?**

SECTION 3: In Family

 Personal Illustration: The Apple Doesn't Fall Far from the Tree
I knew Tim, the husband in the letter, quite well. Tim was my boss for over thirteen years in a mission we grew together. He was a man of God who taught and modeled the importance of living and preaching grace to yourself and others. Along with my wife, Jill, Tim was the single most impactful person in my life for good. I know all this because "Tim" was my father, Jack Miller. My mom had given me a copy of this letter; in fact, she'd passed it out for others to read. We published it in our mission's newsletter out of our desire to be a community that embodied the gospel. But I didn't notice these patterns in my dad's life—likely because Dad and I shared the same idolatry! My idolatry had a different shape to it. I wanted to lead and grow a mission with a million dollars in revenue. Years later, when I saw and confessed to Jill this love of ministry-for-Jesus more than love of Jesus, she said, "The apple doesn't fall far from the tree!"

Repentance from Idols
Ministry idolatry erases Jesus at the center of life and makes ministry for Jesus an alternative source of life.

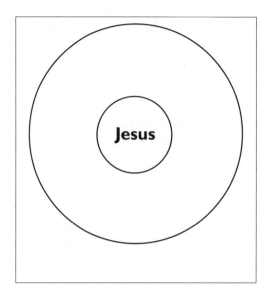

Gospel Connection: Repentance

- Repentance involves moving from "in Family" or "in Ministry" to "in Christ."
- Repentance is ongoing; it's a lifestyle.

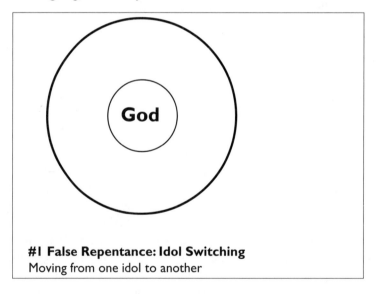

#1 False Repentance: Idol Switching
Moving from one idol to another

Two "False Repentances":
False Repentance #1, Idol Switching:[4]

---

[4] This "idol-switching" idea comes from Keller, *Counterfeit Gods*.

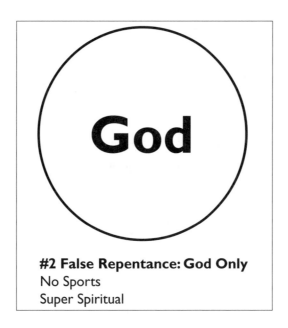

#2 False Repentance: God Only
No Sports
Super Spiritual

False Repentance #2, "God Only":

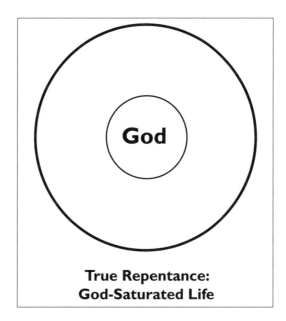

True Repentance:
God-Saturated Life

True Repentance, God Saturated: When God is at the center, then our loves are "rightly ordered."

Personal Illustration: Family Boasting

Every family has "boasts." They are often clues to what false loves (the Flesh) dominate our lives. As Jill and I reflected on our families, here are some of the "boasts" that we each brought into our marriage. Each "boast" is a clue to something we worship.

Paul Miller's Family Boasts
1. Church Work: "Our church is special."
2. Family Unique: "We are tough. We are unique. Where others fail, we come through."
3. Intellectual Pride: "We're smart. We can talk about any subject. We're creative."

Jill Miller's Family Boasts
1. Work: "Do it now. Nail it."
2. Finances: "We are thrifty. We save. We don't spend foolishly."
3. Clean: "They should be more organized."

LESSON 4 APPLICATION

Family Idol Research

1. What are some of your family's idol patterns?

My Mom's Family Idols:

a.

b.

c.

My Dad's Family Idols:

a.

b.

c.

My Idols:

Some questions to help you with your list above:
a. What do you prize?
b. What do you judge?
c. What little sayings or advice does your family pass down or talk about?
d. Where do you spend your free time?
e. What consumes your mental energies?

f. What are you addicted to?

g. What do you say "never" about?

Write a letter to yourself

Imagine a trusted friend writing a letter to you about one area in your life that is a dominant love. What would he or she say? Remember, this friend values you and wants the best for you. Your letter does not have to be long.

Quiz to Detect Idolatry

If this is convicting for you, let the Holy Spirit use it to make you a better lover of people. The Spirit not only convicts but also gives us the power to become like Jesus. In Lesson 5, we will discover that Paul isn't just exposing false loves; he has a new love, Jesus, at the center of his life. In Lesson 6, we discover the wonder of justification by faith—that the ground of our holiness is Jesus' work for us in his death and resurrection, not our own performance.

Reflect on Family Idolatry

2. How do you handle criticism of family members?

   If you are defensive—"my family, right or wrong"—then you might be worshipping your family.

3. Do you presume that your family members, when attacked by others from the outside, are in the right?

4. Are you willing to talk to a family member about sin in their life and risk their rejection of you?

If not, you are prizing family and relationships above God's righteousness.

5. Are there ways that you boast in your family or lift your family above other families?

6. What do you judge other people or families for?

That can be a clue as to what your prize or idol is in your own family.

7. Do you think of your family as special or unique?

8. Do you ever compare your family with other families in terms of appearance, money, or success?

9. Have you ever been willing to do something that risks your family for the kingdom? For example, have you encouraged a child to become a missionary (that will separate your family), given away a large sum of money (that will weaken your family's future), or confronted a family member with sin (that could divide your family)?

10. If God has blessed your family, do you secretly believe it is because you are special or have worked harder than others have? That is, do you believe God's blessing on your family is because of his grace or your work?

11. Do you saturate your family with prayer because you know how needy your family is?

12. Do you favor family members who are wealthier or more successful over ones that are less so?

Reflect on Work Idolatry

13. Do you work 24/7? If you have trouble stopping work (even mentally), you could be idolizing work.

14. Do you inwardly compare your salary with other people's salary?

15. Are you honest at work in such a way that you might risk your job or a future promotion? Or are you a people pleaser at work, trying to get ahead?

16. In meetings and emails, are you quick to encourage other people or to give other people credit?

17. Do you enjoy the fun of competition or does winning become life for you?

Reflect on Ministry Idolatry

18. When you are with someone, do you focus on them and their needs or how they might fit into or hear about your ministry?

19. How do you react when someone leaves your ministry?

20. How do you react when someone criticizes your ministry?

21. Do you pray for other ministries? Do you hope and work for their success?
    Loving other ministries, wishing them the best, is a great antidote to idolizing your own ministry.

22. When another similar church or ministry prospers more than yours, do you rejoice with their success? What is your gut reaction?

"Rejoicing with those who rejoice" is Jesus' hardest command for many ministry leaders because it requires your death to the triumph of your ministry.

23. Do you value people as people—listening to them, caring for them, regardless of whether they attend your church, ministry, etc.?

When we idolize our ministry, we love people as long as they are involved in our ministry and functioning well. If we idolize our ministry, then we use people. They are valuable only as they feed our idol. Once they stop feeding our idol, we can quietly discard them.

24. Are you just as excited that your ministry is attracting needy people as you are mature leaders?

Notice how balanced Jesus is between needy people and mature leaders.

25. Do you cultivate any hidden ministries that have nothing to do with your public ministry—things that you don't tell anyone about, that you do just for Jesus? In other words, what do you do simply because you love Jesus?

There is no greater test of whether your ministry is an idol than this. In Matthew 6:1-18, Jesus goes after our tendency to turn ministry into a show by calling us to make our ministries of fasting, prayer, and giving hidden.

26. Do you actively work to de-center yourself, to encourage others in your ministry to flourish? Do you actively mentor young men or women to lead a future generation?

The activity of de-centering yourself, making space for the Spirit and others not only helps the ministry flourish, but it is also a sign that your ego is not tied up with the success of the ministry.

27. What consumes you—ministry for Jesus or Jesus himself?

It is a subtle but important difference. The first can be idolatry and the second love.

28 Are those closest to you neglected because of your involvement in ministry?

Idolatry always sacrifices those you love on its altar. Death is always at the center of love.

Detect Ministry Idolatry *(For Pastors and Church Leaders)*

29. Do you bless and enjoy people who leave your church or ministry?

30. Do you rank yourself with other teachers or leaders by number of people or money?

31. What priority is personal prayer and praying together?

    If your work is not saturated with prayer, then likely you are unknowingly putting yourself, human wisdom, or money at the center of your ministry.

32. If you have wealthy or powerful people supporting your work, have you ever been afraid to speak to them about issues in their lives because you feared losing their money or influence?

33. What is one insight you have had from your study today that you'd like to hang onto in the week to come?

LESSON 5: IN LOVE

SECTION 1: Paul's Loss and Gain

Philippians 3:3-9

3 For we are "the circumcision," who worship by the Spirit of God and *boast* in Christ Jesus and not in the flesh putting confidence—4 though I myself have reason for confidence in the flesh also. If anyone else thinks he has reason for confidence in the flesh, I have more:

5 circumcised on the eighth day,
of the people of Israel,
of the tribe of Benjamin,
a Hebrew of Hebrews;
as to the law, a Pharisee;
6 as to zeal, a persecutor of the church;
as to righteousness under the law, blameless.

7 But whatever gain I had, I counted as loss for the sake of Christ. 8 Indeed, I count everything as loss because of the surpassing worth of knowing Christ Jesus my Lord. For his sake I have suffered the loss of all things and count them as rubbish, in order that I may gain Christ 9 and be found in him, not having a righteousness of my own that comes from the law, but that which comes through faith in Christ, the righteousness from God that depends on faith.

1. Summarize Paul's thinking in verses 7 and 8.

2. What pattern do you see in verses 7 and 8?

	IN ISRAEL: PAUL'S LOSS	IN CHRIST: PAUL'S GAIN
1st	[7] But whatever gain I had, I counted as loss. . .	for the sake of Christ.
2nd	[8] Indeed, I count everything as loss. . .	because of the surpassing worth of knowing Christ Jesus my Lord.
3rd	For his sake I have suffered the loss of all things and count them as rubbish. . .	in order that I may gain Christ and [9] be found in him, not having a righteousness of my own that comes from the law, but that which comes through faith in Christ, the righteousness from God that depends on faith—

3. What happens to his emotional intensity on the loss side of the chart?

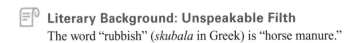 **Literary Background: Unspeakable Filth**

The word "rubbish" (*skubala* in Greek) is "horse manure."

4. What emotional pattern do you see in Paul on the right side of the chart?

5. What does Paul's attitude towards his loss have in common with his gain?

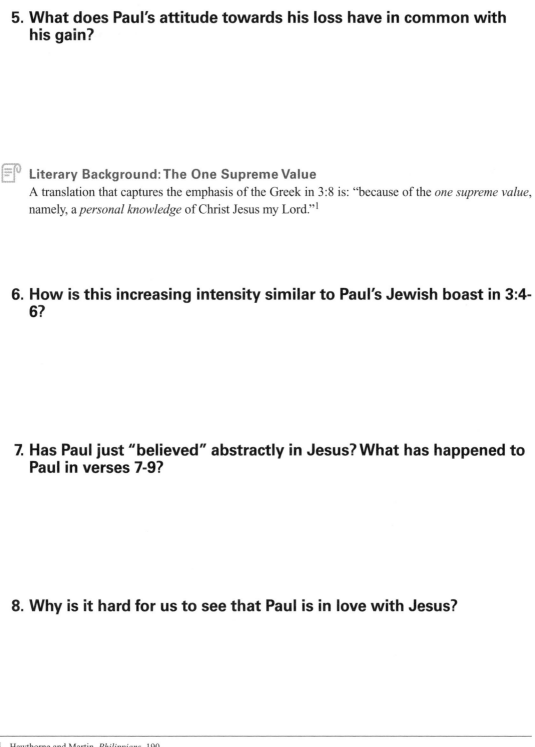

Literary Background: The One Supreme Value

A translation that captures the emphasis of the Greek in 3:8 is: "because of the *one supreme value*, namely, a *personal knowledge* of Christ Jesus my Lord."[1]

6. How is this increasing intensity similar to Paul's Jewish boast in 3:4-6?

7. Has Paul just "believed" abstractly in Jesus? What has happened to Paul in verses 7-9?

8. Why is it hard for us to see that Paul is in love with Jesus?

---

[1] Hawthorne and Martin, *Philippians*, 190.

Literary Background: Hebrew Way of Knowing

Philippians 3 is about *knowing* Jesus. For Jews such as Paul, *knowing* (yada) was personal and intimate.[2] You didn't know abstractly but you entered a person's life.

 Modern Culture: We See Sin but Not Love

Since the Reformation, the church has been good at seeing sin and idols but has (in general) struggled to see and celebrate love.

9. How does this change how we think of union with Christ, of being "in Jesus"?

 Personal Illustration: Counting Money Rubbish

Growing up in California, our family was rich in faith but low on money. My father, Jack Miller, was a Christian schoolteacher and pastor of a small church. He always had a second job to make ends meet. We never asked for things when we went to the store. Once a month when dad got his paycheck, we'd eat out at A&W Root Beer.

We moved to Philadelphia in 1964, and after college, I began working in inner city Christian schools. My starting salary was $6,600 per year so, like my dad, I painted houses and did tax preparation in the evenings and weekends. We expanded the tax business, opening a second tax office, which was quickly profitable. With a growing family, the prospect of making money was mildly intoxicating. I began to think of leaving the inner city and expanding our tax business. There was nothing wrong with making money, but money had captured my heart, becoming my "confidence in the Flesh."

Then in December 1981, God gave us the gift of Kimberly. Of course, at first it didn't seem like a gift. In fact, having a daughter affected by significant disabilities gave our world a grayish cast. Sadness entered our home and settled in for a long stay. Looking back, God was reordering our loves. We were dying to old desires as new ones began to emerge. Overnight my desire to be wealthy vaporized. I became hungry for God. What I formerly counted as a gain, I now considered a loss.

---

[2] Hawthorne and Martin, *Word Biblical Commentary: Philippians*, 191.

10. First Paul says, "I counted as loss," then "I count." What is the time difference?

11. Where is Paul (past, present, or future) when he says, "that I may gain Christ and be found in him, not having . . . "?

	IN ISRAEL: PAUL'S LOSS	IN CHRIST: PAUL'S GAIN
1st	7 But whatever gain I *had*, I *counted* as loss. . .	for the sake of Christ.
2nd	8 Indeed, I *count* everything as loss. . .	because of the surpassing worth of *knowing* Christ Jesus my Lord.
3rd	For his sake I have *suffered* the loss of all things and *count* them as rubbish. . .	in order that I *may gain* Christ and 9 *be found* in him, not having a righteousness of my own that comes from the law, but that which *comes* through faith in Christ, the righteousness from God that *depends* on faith—

Personal Illustration: Falling in Love With Jesus

The letter in Lesson 4 from Janet to Tim was a letter from my mom, Rose Marie Miller, to my dad, Jack Miller. Some seven years later God began to deal with my own idol of ministry in two ways. Negatively, he began to slowly take away from me the ministry that I loved. Positively, he began to give me a new love for Jesus. He did that by putting Jill under enormous pressure. Life was already hard with six kids and a tight mission's salary, but a child with multiple disabilities was the tipping point. Jill began to doubt my love for her. She questioned me with the same boldness and love that my mom had challenged my dad with by asking me, "Do you love me?" After initially recoiling from Jill's doubting my love for her, the Spirit began to give me a hunger to understand love. I suspected I could discover what love was by studying the person of Jesus.

The month after Jill's challenge to me, I began immersing myself in the Gospels with the question, "What is love?" I was transfixed by Jesus—by how he looked at people, how compassionate he was, how he valued people instead of being a ministry-healing-machine. I noticed how much more efficient I was than Jesus.

Since that sabbatical, I have repeatedly tried to get the church to share my passion for the person of Jesus. First I created *The Love Course*. Then I wrote an interactive Bible study, *Person of Jesus*. In 1999, I started a ministry called seeJesus. In 2001, I wrote a book, *Love Walked Among Us*. Next I tried pastors' conferences ('03), *Person of Jesus* Seminars ('04), and started a network of trainers ('06). God blessed these efforts, but none of them penetrated the church's mind. I get multiple invitations to speak on prayer each year, but none on the person of Jesus. I've not been able to get the church to look at him—the glowing center of our faith. I've often argued with God, "Why haven't you done this? Don't you want your church to see your Son?"

I keep trying. One of our missing pieces has been the lack of leadership for our *Person of Jesus* work. In 2014, my board chair called me with a possible lead, a former executive with Prison Fellowship. I cleared my schedule and headed off to Virginia. My lower back ached as I drove through Maryland. It was a long drive for a seeming long shot. I wondered, "Why do I keep throwing myself at this unmovable barrier? Why do I keep recruiting, writing, and praying? Am I in denial?" Sometimes God just closes the door. I didn't want to be stubborn. Then it dawned on me. I'm not in denial; I'm in love! I love Jesus. That love compels me to pick myself up after each seeming failure, dust myself off, and throw myself yet one more time at this goal of getting the church to embrace the person of Jesus. Great loves allow you to endure.

Recently, I was in Ireland doing a seminar, and I met an Irish leader at a pub. I thought, "How do I explain myself simply, without pretense?" So I told him, "I love Jesus." I realized it sounded strange, maybe even pietistic or overly spiritual, but that's okay. Great loves win the day. They did at Calvary.

Another person who loved Jesus was St. Patrick, who brought Ireland to faith. For years I carried his prayer in my wallet and would frequently read it.

> Christ be with me, Christ within me, Christ behind me, Christ before me, Christ beside me, Christ to win me, Christ to comfort and restore me. Christ beneath me, Christ above me, Christ in quiet, Christ in danger, Christ in hearts of all that love me, Christ in mouth of friend and stranger.

St. Patrick was in love with Jesus. I am too.

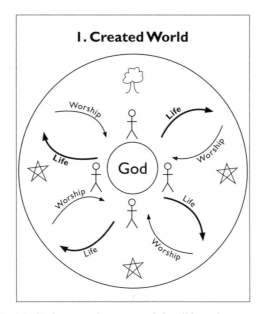

1. **In the Created World**, God was at the center giving life and we returned thanks.

2. **In the Fallen World**, we erased God and created idols (false sources of life).

C. S. Lewis said:

> What Satan put into the heads of our remote ancestors was the idea that they could "be like gods"—could set up on their own as if they had created themselves—be their own masters—invent some sort of happiness for themselves outside God, apart from God. And out of that hopeless attempt has come nearly all that we call human history—money, poverty, ambition, war, prostitution, classes, empires, slavery—the long terrible story of man trying to find something other than God which will make him happy. God cannot give us a happiness and peace apart from Himself, because it is not there. There is no such thing.[3]

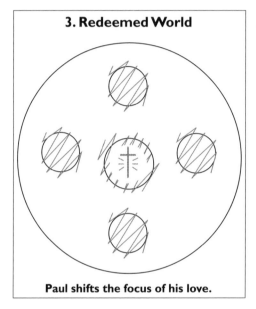

3. Redeemed World

Paul shifts the focus of his love.

3. **In the Redeemed World**, Paul looks back at his false center of life (obedience to the law) and calls it rubbish. Paul dies to his old false source of life and discovers in the cross a new, restored source of life. His love moved from creature back to the creator.

---

[3] Lewis, *Mere Christianity*, 53-54.

LESSON 5 APPLICATION

Reflect on Gains and Losses

1. Can you think of something that you at one time prized but later came to consider a loss, even rubbish? Tell the story below.

2. Share your stories with one another. What common patterns do you see in those stories?

Reflect on Loving Jesus

3. How does it feel to say, "I love Jesus"?

4. Do you love Jesus?

5. Have you ever told anyone that you love Jesus?

6. If it was uncomfortable for you to say, "I love Jesus," why do you think that is?

Reflect on Sentimentality

Peter Kreeft wrote:

> Bernard of Clairvaux, a Doctor of the Church and a great lover of God, said that when he looked at a crucifix, the wounds of Christ seemed like lips speaking to him and saying, "I love you." Everything is like that. Everything is God's lips speaking love, God's message to us. Everything has its meaning here between God and us, not in itself. Everything is relative to this absolute.

7. Is Bernard of Clairvaux overly sentimental when he reflects, "the wounds of Christ seemed like lips speaking to him and saying, 'I love you'"?

Church History: Medieval Church in Love With Jesus

Beginning with Bernard of Clairvaux (1090-1153), the Middle Ages saw an outpouring of love for the person of Jesus and particularly his birth and Passion. Like all movements, this one had its weaknesses: 1) it got stuck on either the baby Jesus or the dying Jesus and not on his resurrection; 2) it confused our suffering with Jesus' suffering, thinking incorrectly that our suffering paid for our sins; and 3) at times, it became too sentimental.[4] Sentimentalism takes a feeling about love ("falling

---

[4] For an example of Medieval sentimentality, a Franciscan monk wrote, "Kiss the beautiful little feet of the infant Jesus who lies in the manger and beg his mother to offer to let you hold him a while. Pick him up and hold him in your arms. Gaze on his face with devotion and reverently kiss and delight in him." https://www.metmuseum.org/toah/hd/priv/hd_priv.htm

in love") and makes it overly dramatic. Intense feelings of love are not wrong. Jesus has intense feelings of love as his heart breaks over Jerusalem's rejection of him (Luke 13:34-35, 19:41-42).

At the same time, the medieval church's love for Jesus was a genuine work of the Spirit. Francis of Assisi (1181-1226), another lover of Jesus, founded the Franciscans and gave us the first-ever Christmas manger scene. Classics such as Thomas a Kempis' *The Imitation of Christ* (1418) come from this time.

Are we afraid to say that we love Jesus? Are we afraid of being pegged as sentimental? Three times Jesus asks Peter by the Sea of Galilee, "Do you love me?" Three times Peter replies, "I love you." Are we afraid to say out loud that we love Jesus? Partly as a reaction against sentimentality, it is rare for a pastor to say he loves Jesus. Not my dad. He used to ask people, "Have you ever done anything because you love Jesus?"

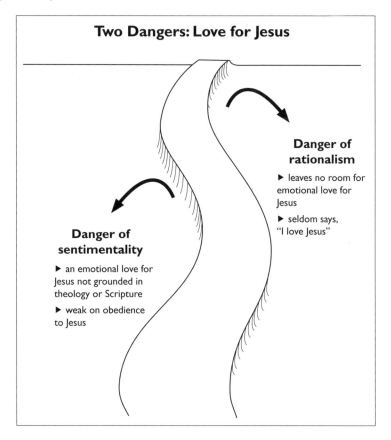

Two Dangers: Love for Jesus

Danger of rationalism
▶ leaves no room for emotional love for Jesus
▶ seldom says, "I love Jesus"

Danger of sentimentality
▶ an emotional love for Jesus not grounded in theology or Scripture
▶ weak on obedience to Jesus

8. Which of these dangers is more real to you? How do you know?

More Reflections on Gains and Losses

JESUS' COMMAND[5]	WHAT I LOSE	WHAT I GAIN
"Love your enemies."	The joy of revenge.	My soul. Freedom from bitterness. My enemy becomes my friend.
"Forgive as you have been forgiven."	Justice.	A quiet heart and mind. The knowledge that I, too, am forgiven.
"Repent and sin no more."	The fleeting pleasure of sin.	The joy of repentance. Freedom from the destructive power of sin.
"When you have a feast, invite the poor and the lame."	Peace and quiet.	The sheer joy of making the poor and disabled part of my life! Friends!
"Take up your cross and follow me."	The emptiness of a pleasure-seeking life.	The joy of a life of love and fellowship with Jesus and my other cross-bearers.

9. What strikes or convicts you about this chart? Which commands are hardest for you to obey?

10. What is one insight you've had from your study today that you'd like to hold onto in the week to come?

---

[5] Chart contributed by John White, Purcellville, VA.

Unit 1: United With Christ

PART 2:
JUSTIFICATION BY FAITH

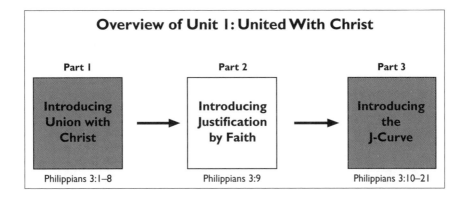

LESSON 6: LIBERATING THE SELF

Philippians 3:7-9

> [7] But whatever gain I had, I counted as loss for the sake of Christ. [8] Indeed, I count everything as loss because of the surpassing worth of knowing Christ Jesus my Lord. For his sake I have suffered the loss of all things and count them as rubbish, in order that I may gain Christ [9] and be found in him, not having a righteousness of my own that comes from the law, but that which comes through faith in Christ, the righteousness from God that depends on faith—

 Literary Insight: A-B-B-A Pattern

Below is the Greek word order for 3:9. In this A-B-B-A pattern, the matching parts (A and A', B and B') are in tension with one another.[1] The most important part of an A-B-B-A pattern is the center. An equivalent phrase from Paul for "a righteousness of my own that comes from the law" is "works of the law."[2]

    A Not having my righteousness
        B the one out of the law
   C but the one through faith in Christ
        B' the one of God
    A'   righteousness upon faith.

ABB'A' patterns were common in the ancient Near East. Jesus frequently uses ABB'A'.

        A The Sabbath was made
          B for man,
          B' not man
        A' for the Sabbath.

---

[1] Silva, *Philippians*, 160.

[2] See Appendix for further information.

1. What are the two kinds of righteousness Paul contrasts in 3:9?

2. What is Paul referring to when he says "a righteousness of my own that comes from the law"?

 Personal Illustration: A Fresh Look at Justification by Faith

In the spring, following the birth of our daughter Kim in December 1981, my dad invited me to a Bible study. Dad never particularly cared how many people showed up—he loved the work of creating disciples and knew it usually started small. A handful of us met in the garage behind his house. At our first meeting we read Martin Luther's introduction to his *Commentary on the Book of Galatians* (1535). I was transfixed. I remember coming home, putting Luther's introduction on the kitchen table and telling Jill, "If the church really got this, it would change things." Luther introduced me to the gospel in a fresh way. I knew the implications of justification by faith for salvation, but I'd not thought about the implications of justification for sanctification (the process of becoming like Jesus). I sensed this was a game changer.

SECTION 2: Luther's Rediscovery

Church History: Luther and the Reformation

As much as the medieval church loved Jesus, it confused Jesus' sufferings with our sufferings. Martin Luther was a monk who in 1517 rediscovered Paul the apostle's teaching of justification by faith. Prior to this, Luther thought he had to confess and pay for his sins in order for God to be pleased with him. He believed that Jesus' suffering plus his own suffering paid for his sins. The result was an agony of conscience and soul. He was never sure he had done enough penance or confession. The "righteousness of God" made him angry because he thought it was an impossible goal.[3] Through studying Romans, Luther realized the righteousness of God was a gift received through Christ's atonement. Once Luther rediscovered justification by faith, he realized that he was "justified by his blood" (Romans 5:9), not by what he did. That began the Protestant Reformation.[4]

The following is Luther's description of justification by faith taken from his preface to his commentary on Galatians.

1) ". . . for there are various sorts of righteousness. There is political or civil righteousness, which emperors, princes of this world . . . deal with. There is ceremonial righteousness, which human traditions teach. This righteousness may be taught without danger by parents and schoolteachers

---

[3] Paul's phrase "the righteousness of God" has multiple nuances. A good summary is by Moo, *The Epistle to the Romans*, 79-90 and 218-243.

[4] A simple explanation of justification: "At his conversion, he [Paul] had to drop the notion that he and God were partners in the project of justification and to accept the means of righteousness that God alone provided," Thielman, *Philippians*, 170.

because they do not attribute to it any power to satisfy for sin, to please God, or to deserve grace; but they teach such ceremonies as are necessary simply for the correction of manners . . . . Besides these, there is another righteousness, called the righteousness of the law or the Ten Commandments, which Moses teaches. We too teach this, according to the doctrine of faith."[5]

2) ". . . There is yet another righteousness that is above all these—namely the righteousness of faith . . . . We do nothing in this matter; we give nothing to God but simply receive and allow someone else to work in us—that is, God."[6]

3) "But human weakness and misery is so great in the terrors of conscience and danger of death, we see nothing but our works, our unworthiness, and the law . . . . the afflicted and troubled conscience has no remedy against desperation and eternal death unless it takes hold of the forgiveness of sins by grace, freely offered in Christ Jesus . . . . Thus I abandon all active righteousness, both of my own and of God's law, and embrace only that passive righteousness that is the righteousness of grace, mercy, and forgiveness of sins . . . ."[7]

4) "I am indeed a sinner, as far as this present life and righteousness are concerned, as I am a child of Adam; where the law accuses me, death reigns over me and wants to ultimately devour me. But I have another righteousness and live above this life—Christ the Son of God, who knows no sin or death but is righteousness and eternal life . . . ."[8]

3. How does Luther feel about his relationship with God prior to realizing his justification by faith?

4. How does justification by faith fit the idea that "all of life is gift"?

---

[5] Luther, *Galatians*, xvii.

[6] Ibid.

[7] Ibid., xviii.

[8] Ibid., xxi.

◎ **Gospel Connection: More Than Forgiveness**

Justification by faith is the core benefit of the gospel that means two things: we are completely forgiven and we are counted completely righteous.[9]

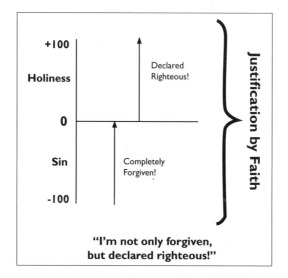

"I'm not only forgiven, but declared righteous!"

SECTION 3: The Problem with Righteousness-by-Doing

5. What is the problem with getting righteousness from righteous deeds?

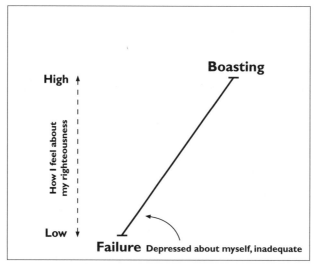

---

[9]   See Gaffin, *By Faith, Not by Sight*, 50-57, for a clear and helpful summary of justification by faith.

Jeremiah 17:9

The heart is deceitful above all things, and desperately sick; who can understand it?

⊚ Gospel Connection: What Corrupts Us?

A corrupt heart with a moral purpose never achieves perfection. Luther said we are "curved in" on ourselves:

> Our nature, by the corruption of the first sin, [being] so deeply curved in on itself that it not only bends the best gifts of God towards itself and enjoys them . . . or rather even uses God himself in order to attain these gifts, but it also fails to realize that it so wickedly, curvedly, and viciously seeks all things, even God, for its own sake.[10]

The only way to undercut human pride (and despair) was to separate righteousness from the human ego. Righteousness had to become a gift!

SECTION 4: Paul and Luther: Boasting and Failure

6. How does justification by faith speak to both failure and boasting?

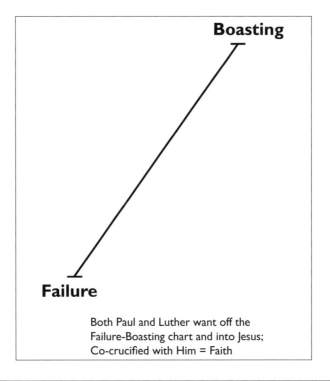

Boasting

Failure

Both Paul and Luther want off the
Failure-Boasting chart and into Jesus;
Co-crucified with Him = Faith

---

[10] Johnston, *Saving God: Religion After Idolatry*, 88. Luther's Latin phrase was *incurvatus in se*.

🕖 **Historical Background: Martin Luther**

In contrast to Paul, Luther was not happy. But the gospel applies both to Paul's boasting and Luther's despair. Both the proud heart and the despairing heart need justification by faith.[11]

7. How might despair of our Flesh and confidence in our Flesh be similar?

SECTION 5: Pharisee and Tax Collector

Philippians 3:4-6

—[4] though I myself have reason for confidence in the flesh also. If anyone else thinks he has reason for confidence in the flesh, I have more: [5] circumcised on the eighth day, of the people of Israel, of the tribe of Benjamin, a Hebrew of Hebrews; as to the law, a Pharisee; [6] as to zeal, a persecutor of the church; as to righteousness under the law, blameless.

Luke 18:9-14

[9] He [Jesus] also told this parable to some who trusted in themselves that they were righteous, and treated others with contempt: [10] "Two men went up into the temple to pray, one a Pharisee and the other a tax collector. [11] The Pharisee, standing by himself, prayed thus: 'God, I thank you that I am not like other men, extortioners, unjust, adulterers, or even like this tax collector. [12] I fast twice a week; I give tithes of all that I get.' [13] But the tax collector, standing far off, would not even lift up his eyes to heaven, but beat his breast, saying, 'God, be merciful to me, a sinner!' [14] I tell you, this man went down to his house justified, rather than the other. For everyone who exalts himself will be humbled, but the one who humbles himself will be exalted."

8. What are the similarities between the Pharisee and the In-the-Law Paul?

---

[11] See Appendix: Lesson Note 5.

Unit 1: United With Christ

9. What similarities do you see between the tax collector and the In-Jesus Paul?

10. How does the tax collector break through to God?

11. Look back at Philippians 3:9. How does the new In-Christ Paul break through to God? What is Paul's one-word description?

12. What is the relationship between faith and boasting?

13. Put this parable together with Paul's faith that he mentions twice in 3:9. What is faith, at its very simplest?

14. What happens to both the tax collector and Paul because they have faith?

LESSON 6 APPLICATION

Scholar Peter Kreeft: The Gift of Love Is Ours for the Taking

I am a Roman Catholic. But the most liberating idea I have ever heard I learned from Martin Luther. Pope John Paul II told the German Lutheran bishops that Luther was profoundly right about this idea. He said that Catholic teaching affirms it just as strongly and that there was no contradiction between Protestant and Catholic theology on this terribly important point that was the central issue of the Protestant Reformation.[12] I speak, of course, about "justification by faith" and its consequence, which Luther called "Christian liberty" or "the liberty of a Christian" in his little gem of an essay by that name.

Let's begin with a solid certainty: God is love. God is a lover. He is not a manager, businessman, accountant, owner, or puppet-master. What he wants from us first of all is not a technically correct performance but our heart. Protestants and Catholics alike need to relearn or re-emphasize that simple, liberating truth. When I first read C.S. Lewis' statement of it in *Mere Christianity* . . . it liberated me just as it had the Catholic Augustinian monk Luther 450 years earlier. The crucial sentence for me was: "We may think God wants actions of a certain kind, but God wants people of a certain sort."

The point is amazingly simple, which is why so many of us just don't get it. Heaven is free because love is free. It's a gift for the taking. The taking is faith. "If you believe, you will be saved." It's really that simple. If I offer you a gift, you have it if and only if you have the faith to take it.

The primacy of faith does not discount or denigrate works, but liberates them. Our good works can now also be free—free from the worry and slavery and performance anxiety of having to buy heaven with them. Our good works can now flow from genuine love of neighbor, not fear of hell. Nobody wants to be loved merely as a means to build up the lover's merit pile. That attempt is ridiculous logically as well as psychologically. How much does heaven cost? A thousand good works? Would 999 not do, then? The very question shows its own absurdity. That absurdity comes from forgetting that God is love.

God practices what he preaches. He loves the sinner and hates only the sin. The father of the prodigal son did not say to his repentant son: "You are welcome home, son, but of course you must now pay me back for all the harm you've done and all the money you've wasted." He didn't even say, "I hope you've learned your lesson." He simply fell on his neck, kissed him, and wept.

The righteous older brother was scandalized by this injustice and justification of the sinner—just as the day-long laborers in another of Christ's strange and wonderful parables were scandalized when the master of the vineyard gave the same wage he had given them to the late arrivals. So too the people who heard Jesus forgive the repentant thief on the cross were probably scandalized by the

---

[12] While the Catholic Church has moved in the direction of Luther, there are still significant differences between Catholic and Protestant theology on justification with Catholic theology tending to merge declared with infused righteousness.

words: "Today you shall be with me in Paradise." They probably thought, "But what about all his past sins? What about justice? What about punishment?" The answer is found in 1 John 4:18: "There is no fear in love, but perfect love casts out fear. For fear has to do with punishment."

God cannot be outdone in loving us lavishly. No one can even imagine how loving God is: "Eye hath not seen, nor ear heard, neither have entered into the heart of man, the things which God hath prepared for them that love him" (1 Cor 2:9 KJV). The prodigal son did not find himself in the servants' quarters but in the banquet hall. He had hoped his father might consent to take him back as one of his hired servants, but he was dressed in festal robes and fed the fatted calf.

The whole point of justification by faith is God's scandalous, crazy, and wonderful gift of love.[13]

1. What insights of Peter Kreeft do you find helpful?

2. How does justification by faith liberate you? What does it liberate you from?

3. Do you tend to boast like the apostle Paul or despair like Luther? Or both?

Reflect on Justification in Your Life

Debbie's Situation: The Sailboat Race

Debbie's son was in a sailboat race. Just before the race started another mother asked Debbie if she could ride with her son on his Sunfish during the race. Without thinking, Debbie said yes. The Sunfish is a small boat and the woman's added weight slowed Debbie's son down, causing him to lose the race. After the race, Debbie was quietly angry. She distanced herself from the women. Debbie's identity was in how her son did in his sports. She was "in sports" or "in family" but not "in Jesus."

Complete this sentence for Debbie: "A righteousness of my own that comes from

_____."

---

[13] Kreeft, Peter. "The Twelve Most Profound Ideas I Have Ever Had." *Peter Kreeft* blog. http://www.peterkreeft.com/topics-more/12-ideas.htm. Accessed December 24, 2014.

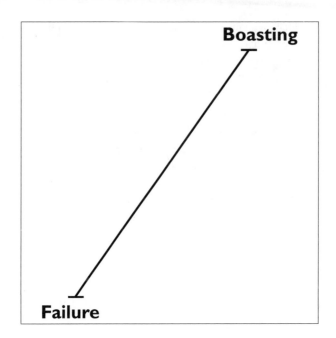

Boasting

Failure

4. Can you write out a story, like Debbie's sailing story, where you were trying to create your own righteousness?

5. What is one insight you've had from your study today that you'd like to hang onto in the week to come?

LESSON 7: DISENTANGLING THE SELF

SECTION 1: The Value of Faith

Philippians 3:7-11

> [7] But whatever *gain* I had, I counted as *loss* for the sake of Christ. [8] Indeed, I *count* everything as *loss* because of the surpassing *worth* of knowing Christ Jesus my Lord. For his sake I have suffered the *loss* of all things and *count* them as rubbish, in order that I may *gain* Christ [9] and be found in him, not having a righteousness of my own that comes from the law, but that which comes through faith in Christ, the righteousness from God that depends on faith—[10] that I may know him and the power of his resurrection, and may share his sufferings, becoming like him in his death, [11] that by any means possible I may attain the resurrection from the dead.

1. **How does the word "faith" feel to you: 1) real, concrete or 2) vague, floaty?**

2. **Look at the words in italics in 3:7-8. What world are we in when Paul talks about *gains*, *losses*, and *count*?**

 Literary Background: Gains and Losses
- Jesus tells Simon a parable of two debtors, one who had been forgiven 500 denarii and one 50 denarii (Luke 7).
- In the Lord's Prayer, Jesus uses "debts" to refer to our sins (Matthew 6).
- Jesus uses it when a servant owes 10,000 talents to the king (Matthew 18).
- Paul says eleven times that God *counts* righteousness to us by faith (Romans 4).

3. **Why is money a good way to describe the gospel?**

Gospel Connection: Money

Paul's terminology is a wonderful way to describe the concreteness of sin and forgiveness.

Modern Culture: How We Create Value

When we think of "faith" we often think of something spiritual or "not real," but our whole world is held together with faith.

Likewise, when our modern culture thinks of faith, it thinks of something vague, without substance. But money is just as vague. It only has value because of our faith in it. Because it is a faith shared by our whole culture, money feels "real."

Our faith in money helps us see how concrete the gospel is.

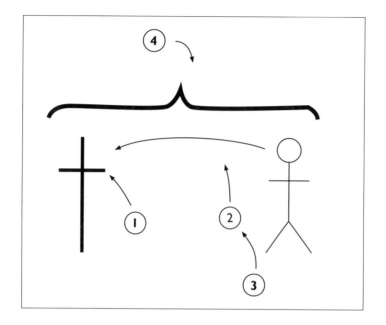

Four Parts to Justification by Faith Chart

    1. **What Jesus does:**

    2. **What I do:**

    3. **What the Spirit does:**

    4. **What the Father does:**

4. What if I don't have enough faith?

Flesh vs. Spirit Chart

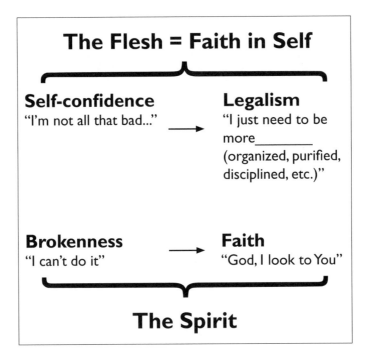

The Flesh = Faith in Self

Self-confidence
"I'm not all that bad..."

Legalism
"I just need to be more_____
(organized, purified, disciplined, etc.)"

Brokenness
"I can't do it"

Faith
"God, I look to You"

The Spirit

Gospel Connection: The Power of Faith

Faith has no energy in itself. It simply looks to Jesus' work on the cross. It is the activity of surrendering. Faith, like the plug for a lamp, connects you to the electricity. It is not the energy, but a conduit for the energy. We mistakenly think that faith is some kind of spiritual energy that we don't have. Remember, the Flesh always begins and ends with itself and its power. Faith is the opposite.

It realizes we can't do life on our own and cries out, "God, be merciful to me, a sinner." Faith is the most powerful thing we do because we realize we can't do anything![1]

5. What's encouraging about the nature of faith?

🎯 **Gospel Connection: The Two Sides of Faith**
- In repentance, you own up to your sin. In faith, you disown your sin because of your union with Christ.
- This is not a formula. We think, "If I get the formula right, I'll be ok, stable, free from care." A formula can take the place of a daily, personal, and real reliance on Jesus. But faith is a personal reliance on the *person* of Jesus Christ. God's best gift is himself.

SECTION 4: The Feelings of Faith

6. What does faith feel like?

A Journey of Faith		
Stage I: Control (No Faith) →	**Stage II** Release Control (Early Faith) →	**Stage III** God's Control (Working Faith)
Self-righteous My rights Fairness is everything	Feels...fearful, alone, vulnerable, unfair, used, helpless, uncertain	Feels...praying, watching, loving, surrendering, hopeful
Self-righteous →	No righteousness →	In-Christ Righteous

---

[1] See Appendix: Lesson Note 6 for additional scholarly reflections.

◎ Gospel Connection: Failure and Faith

Failure and brokenness are the door to faith, but they are not faith. Real faith cries out for grace, like the tax collector. God wants us *off* the Failure-Boasting chart and *in* Jesus.

Quote from "A Letter from Jesus Christ"

John of Landsberg (1542-1591) wrote this devotional using the voice of Jesus:

"I know those moods when you sit there utterly alone, pining, eaten up with unhappiness, in a pure state of grief. You don't move towards me but desperately imagine that everything you have ever done has been utterly lost and forgotten. This near-despair and self-pity are actually a form of pride. What you think was a state of absolute security from which you've fallen was really trusting too much in your own strength and ability . . . what really ails you is that things simply haven't happened as you expected and wanted.

In fact, I don't want you to rely on your own strength and abilities and plans, but to distrust them and to distrust yourself, and to trust me and no one and nothing else. As long as you rely entirely on yourself, you are bound to come to grief. You still have a most important lesson to learn: your own strength will no more help you to stand upright than propping yourself on a broken reed. You must not despair of me. You may hope and trust in me absolutely. My mercy is infinite."[2]

7. What strikes or convicts you from this letter? What is Landsberg's main point?

SECTION 5: The Location of Faith

8. Why can't God justify someone who rejects Jesus?

---

[2] John of Landsberg, *A Letter from Jesus Christ*, 58-59. Obviously, this parable is not the voice of Jesus. This devotional may or may not apply to you. Some depression is simply because our life is depressing. Other depression comes because I'm angry at the life God has given me. Sometimes these are combined. This devotional is focused on the second kind of depression.

9. Where did Paul discover or get this "righteousness from God"?

⊙ **Gospel Connection: Faith**

Faith isn't something we do outside of Jesus. It is God's means for drawing us into Jesus.

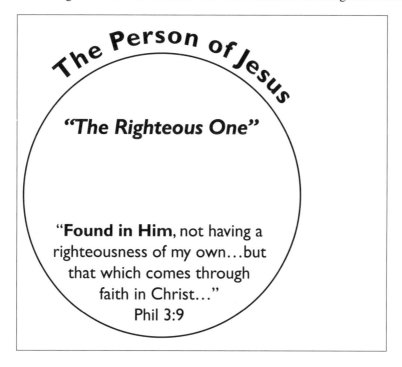

⊙ **Gospel Connection: Union with Christ**

"Justification, according to John Calvin, is not merely an abstract divine declaration with no implication of personal relationship. [3] Calvin writes, 'We do not, therefore, contemplate him outside ourselves from afar in order that his righteousness may be imputed to us but because we put on Christ and are engrafted into his body—in short, because he stoops to make us one with him.'" [4]

If you separate justification by faith from being in Christ, it can feed a spirit of independence. We can use the gospel merely to feel good about ourselves.

---

[3] John Calvin and Martin Luther were the central leaders of the Protestant Reformation in the early 1500s. The Reformation led to the split between the Catholic and Protestant Church.

[4] Evans, *Imputation and Impartation*, 35. The thesis of Evans' book is the historical danger of separating justification by faith from union with Christ. Quote from John Calvin from *Institutes of the Christian Religion*, III.11.10.

LESSON 7 APPLICATION

Reflect on Money and Faith

1. What is helpful for you in seeing how Paul and Jesus both use money to describe sin, faith, our debts to God, etc.?

2. What are other things we put faith in without realizing it?

Reflect on Justification by Faith

3. What did you find helpful about the Justification by Faith chart? Was anything unclear?

4. Review the Flesh vs. Spirit chart. What is helpful about seeing that faith is not some spiritual energy?

5. Why is it helpful to see that you actually do something in salvation?

6. At the same time, what enables us "to do"?

7. Do we look to our justification or to Jesus' work for us on the cross? What is the danger of looking to our justification?

8. What is the danger of separating justification by faith from being in Christ?

Reflect on the Two Sides of Faith

9. How do you find the two sides of faith helpful?

10. Why is it encouraging that faith is actually surrendering?

11. What is hard about admitting that we can't do life on our own?

12. What have your personal struggles with faith been? Where have you been confused?

13. How can despair fool us? What is the difference between despair and faith?

14. What is one insight you've had from your study today that you'd like to hang onto in the week to come?

LESSON 8: DEFENDING THE SELF

Philippians 3:7-9

> [7] But whatever gain I had, I counted as loss for the sake of Christ. [8] Indeed, I count everything as loss because of the surpassing worth of knowing Christ Jesus my Lord. For his sake I have suffered the loss of all things and count them as rubbish, in order that I may gain Christ [9] and be found in him, not having a righteousness of my own that comes from the law, but that which comes through faith in Christ, the righteousness from God that depends on faith—

 Personal Illustration: Good Husband-Righteousness

When our son Andrew was three, he would often ask in the middle of the night for a drink of water. I'd stumble out of bed to the bathroom, pull a Dixie cup from the dispenser and bring it to Andrew. Often, several hours later he would ask for a second cup. After a couple of months, it occurred to me that I could get two Dixie cups—one for now and one for later—and avoid a second trip. The only problem with my little system was that Dixie cups sweat, so the second cup would leave a stain on Andrew's dresser. Jill asked me not to bring the second Dixie cup. So I said, "OK" and brought just one Dixie cup. That's what good husbands do.

One morning several months later just after we'd awakened, Jill called from Andrew's bedroom, "Paul you left a Dixie cup on the dresser. Don't leave Dixie cups on the dresser." I stood in the closet where I was dressing thinking, "I only brought one Dixie cup. I didn't leave that Dixie cup!"

I was offended by Jill's bad information (I left the Dixie cup) and the implication (I was the kind of husband who left Dixie cups on dressers). I was about to correct Jill's declaration of me as unrighteous, when I remembered "a righteousness from God based on faith." Thinking about the gospel helped me realize that my quickness to correct Jill's opinion of me as someone who doesn't remember her concerns was a form of self-righteousness. It is entirely appropriate to defend ourselves from false accusations—Jesus and Paul do it frequently—but what struck me was my *rush* to defend myself, the passion of my planned defense over a silly Dixie cup! I didn't want a vague, detached righteousness from God; I wanted a real righteousness of my own, a righteousness with substance. Jill was declaring me unrighteous and I wanted to be declared righteous! Jill's comment made me feel like I was sliding down the Failure-Boasting scale. I wanted to stop the slide. I wanted my words of justification to anchor me, not God's words of justification.

For the first time in my life—in a real-life mini-drama—standing in our closet, I quietly rested in "a righteousness from God based on faith." The result? I shut up. I didn't defend myself.

What about the Dixie cup? Who left it? I'm actually not sure. It was likely me. Jill never got Dixie cups and either I did it sleep walking or it was the original cup I got the first time I got up. But the real answer is, "Who cares??" That's what faith does. It gets you in the right location.

1. What similarities are there between Paul Miller's Good Husband-Righteousness and Paul the apostle's list of seven boasts?

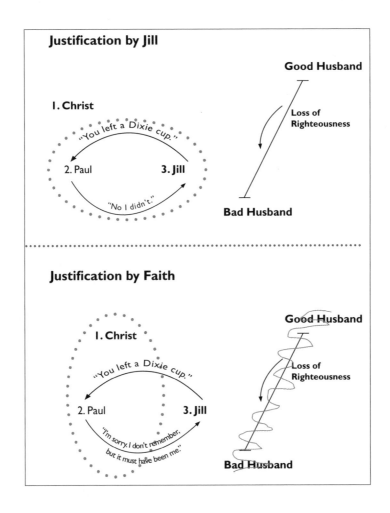

2. Did Paul Miller initially want an earned righteousness ("I didn't leave that Dixie cup") or an unearned righteousness ("a righteousness from God based on faith")? Why?

3. What do we love about an earned righteousness? How does an earned righteousness feel compared with an unearned one?

4. Why are we offended by a righteousness that comes from God by faith?

Gospel Connection: The Impact of Free Righteousness

The primary fruit of "righteousness from God received by faith" (Phil. 3:9) is reconciliation with God. We stand before God forgiven and counted righteous because of the blood of Jesus. But justification by faith also affects how I react to my wife saying I left a Dixie cup on the dresser. My new standing before God (vertical), transforms my standing before my spouse (horizontal). If I'm "in Christ," I don't have to be "in Jill."

Chart: My Two Choices – Justification by Faith or Justification by Doing

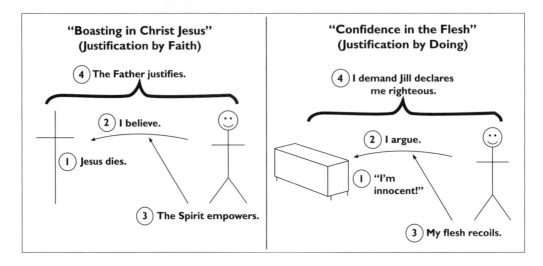

5. Notice the symmetry between justification by faith and justification by Jill. How does each side of the drawing mirror the other?

Luther wrote this about the effect of justification by faith on our behavior:

> When I have this righteousness reigning in my heart . . . I come out into another kingdom, and I do good works whenever I have a chance . . . . If I am a householder, I am in charge of my house and my family, and I bring up my children in the knowledge and fear of God. If I am a magistrate, I work hard at the job that heaven has given me. If I am a servant, I do my master's business faithfully. Whoever is convinced that Christ is his righteousness works cheerfully and well in his vocation . . . .[1]

---

[1] Luther, *Galatians*, xxii.

6. In the story of the Dixie cup, what was the result of Paul Miller believing the gospel? In one word, what kind of response came out of him?

Faith   =>   Love

SECTION 3: Justification by Seinfeld

"Justification" isn't just a religious idea—we all long for justification. That's what Michael Richards is longing for after he flew into a racist rant at a comedy club. Richards, who played the quirky Kramer on "Seinfeld," lost his temper in 2006 when taunted by an African American man in the audience. Here's a summary from the Washington Post:

> Richards, 57, appeared on "Late Show With David Letterman" last night to say he was sorry about his tirade at the Laugh Factory in Hollywood during a stand-up performance. "I lost my temper onstage," he said, adding, "I said some pretty nasty things to some Afro Americans . . . . You know, I'm really busted up over this and I'm very, very sorry."
>
> Footage of the outburst made its way onto the Internet yesterday, prompting the comic actor's response. The clip shows Richards interrupting his monologue onstage and yelling "Shut up!" at a patron, who apparently had been heckling during Richards's routine.
>
> Richards then exploded, "Fifty years ago they'd have you hanging upside down with a [expletive] fork up your [expletive]. Throw his [expletive] out!" He then repeatedly used a crude racial slur to label the man. While some in the audience laughed, one unidentified woman can be heard on a tape of the incident gasping, . . . at the remarks.[2]

The Letterman apology didn't go well. Richards slipped into his comic routine while apologizing, sending a confusing signal to the audience. Seinfeld, who introduced Richards on the show, had to tell the audience to stop laughing. Despite the fact YouTube removed the incriminating video

---

[2] Farhi, Paul. "'Seinfeld' Comic Richards Apologizes for Racial Rant." The Washington Post. Tuesday, November 21, 2006. http://www.washingtonpost.com/wp-dyn/content/article/2006/11/21/AR2006112100242.html

and Seinfeld repeatedly went to bat for him, Richards' shame was so profound he stopped doing stand-up comedy. Seinfeld tried again to redeem his friend by inviting him on his new internet show, "Comedians in Cars Getting Coffee." Seinfeld picks up Richards in an old VW van and they go to get coffee. You can still feel Richards' shame as he tells Seinfeld, "I busted up after that event 7 years ago. It broke me down." Seinfeld encourages Richards to let it go, "Well, that's up to you to say, 'I have been carrying around this bag long enough. I am going to put it down.'" But Richards can't. Sin is too sticky. He just says, "Yeah, yeah."[3]

Richards can't put it down because deep down he knows that he can't justify himself. He instinctively realizes that even Seinfeld with all his goodwill and fame can't declare him righteous. You can't "forgive yourself" because you sinned against a holy God. Only God can forgive. Only God can justify. Only the blood of Christ can satisfy the insatiable thirst of a guilty conscience.

7. How did Richards feel immediately after his tirade? How did he feel seven years later?

8. How does Richards try to alleviate his feelings of shame?

9. When he talks to Seinfeld seven years later, Richards mentions the incident again. Why? What does he want Seinfeld to do?

10. Does Seinfeld declare him righteous? How?

11. Can Seinfeld justify him?

12. Does Richards feel justified by Seinfeld's words?

---

[3] Ibid.

LESSON 8 APPLICATION

Reflect on Stories from This Lesson

1. What are your reflections on the Dixie cup story?

2. What are your reflections on the Richards story?

Writing Your Own Story

3. Think of a single story like Paul Miller's Good Husband-Righteousness story where you were self-righteous. Write it out. Be as detailed as possible.

Share it with your small group.

Think of a simple way to remind yourself throughout the coming week of your In-Christ Righteousness.

4. What is one insight you've had from your study today that you'd like to hang onto in the week to come?

PART 3:
THE J-CURVE

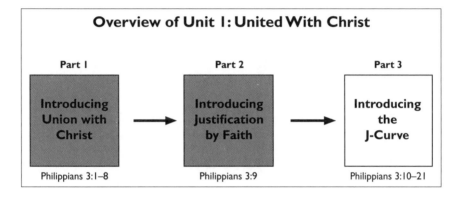

Overview of Unit 1: United With Christ

Part 1		Part 2		Part 3
Introducing Union with Christ	→	Introducing Justification by Faith	→	Introducing the J-Curve
Philippians 3:1–8		Philippians 3:9		Philippians 3:10–21

LESSON 9: SURRENDERING THE SELF

Philippians 3:7-11

> [7] But whatever gain I had, I counted as loss for the sake of Christ.[8] Indeed, I count everything as loss because of the surpassing worth of knowing Christ Jesus my Lord. For his sake I have suffered the loss of all things and count them as rubbish, in order . . .

> that I may gain Christ [9] and be found in him, not having a righteousness of my own that comes from the law, but that which comes through faith in Christ, the righteousness from God that depends on faith—

> [10] that I may know him and the power of his resurrection, and may share his sufferings, becoming like him in his death, [11] that by any means possible I may attain the resurrection from the dead.

1. **Look at 3:10-11. What is different, almost strange about "share his sufferings" and "becoming like him in his death"? What questions do these phrases prompt?**

Personal Illustration: Story of Kayla

Kayla raised money and gave up a week of her time to go work as a short-term missionary at a summer camp for families affected by disability. At the camp, volunteers like Kayla serve the families and those affected by disability. It is hard, but rewarding work. You are part of a team that is embodying the love of Jesus. On the second day of the camp, a mother claimed that Kayla had said something negative about her parenting. The mother went to the camp directors who investigated the allegation. Kayla had no recollection of saying anything. Multiple people were involved, and there was no resolution. On Wednesday, she came to my wife and me completely distraught. We didn't think Kayla had said this, but there was no way of proving it. The camp leadership handled the situation as best they could—but no matter what they did, a cloud hung over Kayla.

2. For Kayla, what does it feel like has happened to her ministry?

⊙ **Gospel Connection: Entering the Gospel**

In fact, Kayla's ministry has gone to a whole new level.

Kayla is now *entering* the gospel; she is entering the path of Christ. So to serve, joyfully, feels like a death to her. It feels like there is no point to love. She is "becoming like him in his death."

She is being humbled. She is going lower. She is losing power. The letter "J" forms the shape of Jesus' life, death, and resurrection. So her life, like Jesus' life, has a shape to it.

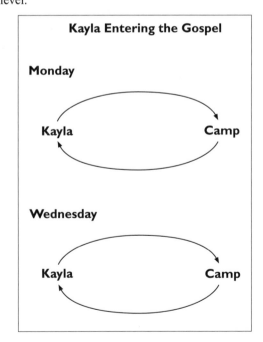

Kayla Entering the Gospel

Monday

Kayla   Camp

Wednesday

Kayla   Camp

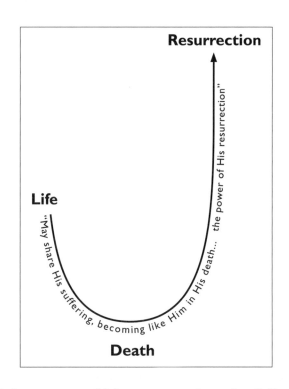

Resurrection

the power of His resurrection"

Life

"May share His suffering, becoming like Him in His death...

Death

3. How might "the power of his resurrection, the fellowship of his sufferings" help Kayla as she serves on Wednesday?

4. What does it do to Kayla's ego and will as she serves on Wednesday, Thursday, and Friday?

5. What dangers does Kayla face (in her soul)? If she doesn't embrace a "fellowship of his sufferings," what might she be tempted by?

Kayla's Choices

Withdrawal
("I'll never come back again.")

Bitterness
(Anger stuffed and leaking)

Kayla

("I ...may share His sufferings")

Anger
(Lashing out)

Gossip
(Creating an alternative community of empathizers)

6. If Kayla embraces this fellowship of his sufferings, what might it do with her relationship with Jesus?

Three Steps to Receiving a Fellowship of His Suffering

1. **See it.**

2. **Receive it.**

3. **Glory in it.**

7. When Paul Miller doesn't defend himself, how might he be entering a mini-fellowship of Jesus' sufferings? What does it cost him?

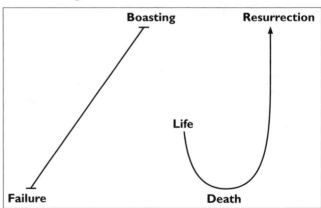

Boasting

Resurrection

Life

Failure

Death

Look closely at 3:10-11.

1st: *A-B-B-A Pattern.* Paul uses the familiar A-B-B'-A' pattern. Matching letters usually mean similar ideas.

> A that I may know him and the power of his resurrection,
>> B and may share his sufferings,
>> B' becoming like him in his death,
> A' that by any means possible I may attain the resurrection from the dead.

8. What is the relationship of death and resurrection?

9. What does this mean for Kayla as she serves for the remaining days of camp?

2nd: *"Share* his sufferings" is "koinonia his sufferings." Koinonia is Paul's favorite word for fellowship. It means an active sharing or participation in Christ's suffering.[1]

10. If Kayla views this rejection as an active sharing in Christ's suffering, then how does that transform her last three days at camp?

---

[1] Bockmuehl, *Philippians*, 215 and O'Brien, *Philippians*, 405. Kevin McFadden: Paul uses *koinonia* to describe his relationship with the Philippians (nouns in 1:5, 7; 2:1; verbs in 4:14, 15).

11. How does it potentially transform Kayla's relationship with the woman who has slandered her?

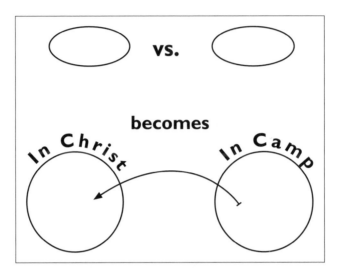

⊙ Gospel Connection: In Christ

Kayla is now "in Christ" instead of being "in Camp." The gospel moves from being something that merely makes her feel good to the very center of her life. By embracing this fellowship, the worst part of the week is completely transformed.

3rd: *Form.* The ESV says "becoming like him in his death." A more literal translation is, "being continually conformed to his death."[2]

1. "continually" means this is an ongoing process.
2. "conformed" means Paul's life is taking the shape or form of Jesus' life.

12. How is Kayla's life taking the form or shape of Jesus' death?

---

[2] "Being continually conformed" is the present, passive verb, *summorphizo*. It appears nowhere else in Greek and is likely coined by Paul from the adjective. The root *morphe* means *"form"* and *"sum"* means *with*. It means "having the same form." The present tense suggests ongoing action. The passive suggests it is being done to Paul. "During his present sufferings Paul is being renewed daily into the image of his Lord, and this means into conformity with his death" (O'Brien, 408).

13. How does it transform your suffering when you see the shape to it?

> **4th:** ***"know him in death and resurrection."*** At first glance, Paul seems to list three ways of knowing Jesus: "that I may 1) know him *and* 2) the power of his resurrection, *and* 3) may share his sufferings." But these aren't three different ways of knowing Jesus. We know him *in* his sufferings.[3] A translation that captures the meaning of verse 10 is:
>
> > "that I may know him *in* the power of his resurrection *in* sharing his sufferings."

14. How does this insight impact Kayla?

15. What is the relationship between knowing Jesus and sharing in his suffering?

> **5th:** *Paul wants this.* It is his passion. He wants to experience Christ's death and resurrection.

16. How does this help Kayla?

17. How might this transform Kayla's mild suffering?

18. Paul wants this, but we recoil from it. Is something wrong with how we've been taught the gospel? What are we missing?

---

[3] Hawthorne and Martin, *Philippians*, 197. Also, O'Brien, *Philippians*, 403. "Clearly the apostle intends to explain what is meant by knowing Christ through this entire phrase [v. 10], and while each expression draws attention to separate facets of knowing him. . . they are nevertheless to be regarded as a single entity."

19. Does "fellowship of his suffering" apply only to Paul the apostle and not to us?

Scholar Richard Gaffin writes, "Sometimes it is argued that the sufferings mentioned . . . [Phil. 3:10-11, 2 Cor. 1:7] are the sufferings of Paul the apostle, specifically apostolic sufferings which exclude the rest of the church. But a number of considerations tell against this restriction: In 2 Corinthians, Paul says that the whole congregation shares in his (Christ's) sufferings. In Philippians, the fellowship of Christ's sufferings and conformity to his death are, along with righteousness by faith, essential aspects of union with Christ . . . Until Christ returns, then, all Christian existence continues to be suffering with Christ."[4]

---

[4]   Gaffin, "The Usefulness of the Cross," 237. "The Usefulness of the Cross" was originally given as an address at Westminster Theological Seminary on April 24, 1979 at the inauguration of Dr. Gaffin as Professor of New Testament. An article first appeared in Westminster Theological Journal 41:1 (Spring 1979) with slight modifications and footnotes.

LESSON 9 APPLICATION

1. What does it cost Paul Miller to not boast?

2. How does the J-Curve help Paul?

Reflect on Your Life

3. Think of a time in your life when you felt unjustly accused like Kayla. What happened? How did you handle it?

4. What did your heart do?

5. If you had been thinking about it as a "fellowship of sharing in his sufferings" how might that have reshaped your reaction?

6. What kind of fellowship or friendship do we like to have? What is our natural response to a "fellowship of his suffering"?

7. What do you *want* out of life? What does it mean that Paul *wants* a "fellowship of his sufferings"? How is Paul different from us? What do you think we are missing?

8. What is one insight you've had from your study today that you'd like to hang onto in the week to come?

LESSON 10: BELIEVE AND BECOME LIKE THE GOSPEL

Philippians 3:7-11[1]

7 But whatever gain I had, I counted as loss for the sake of Christ. 8 Indeed, I count everything as loss because of the surpassing worth of knowing Christ Jesus my Lord. For his sake I have suffered the loss of all things and count them as rubbish, in order

(1) that I may gain Christ 9 and be found in him, not having a righteousness of my own that comes from the law, but that which comes through faith in Christ, the righteousness from God that depends on faith—

(2) 10 that I may know him and the power of his resurrection, and the fellowship of his suffering, taking the form of his death, 11 that by any means possible I may attain the resurrection from the dead.

1. What does Paul mean by the word knowing?

 Literary Background: Knowing Jesus

Paul uses the word *knowing* twice. In Jesus, he knows "a righteousness from God that depends on faith" (verse 9). This is the first way of knowing. He also knows Jesus in a second way, "the

---

1   We've changed "may share his sufferings" to "fellowship of his sufferings." Likewise, we've changed "becoming like him in his death" to "taking the form of his death." See O'Brien, *Philippians*, 408-411.

fellowship of his sufferings" (verse 10). The two sentences parallel one another.[2] Paul gives us two viewpoints of the same person, but when you put the two viewpoints together, you have a richer, more complete whole.

2. How are these two ways of knowing Christ different from how we usually think of knowing him?

3. How are each of these ways of knowing Jesus different? What is the knowing of #1 and what is the knowing of #2?

◎ **Gospel Connection: Two Ways of Knowing**

Both these ways of knowing Jesus for Paul are deeply personal.

Knowing #1: He is in Jesus by faith. He rethinks his whole identity around being in Christ. He rejects an independent life of boasting in himself and boasts in Jesus.

Knowing #2: He is in Jesus by love. He enters into Jesus' suffering and resurrection. He rejects a pleasure-seeking love and self-proclamation and embraces a life of love and shameless proclamation of Jesus. He boasts in his Jesus-like death and resurrection.[3]

4. What are the different ways that Paul is in Jesus in #1 and #2?

Read Philippians 1:29

For it has been granted to you that for the sake of Christ you should not only believe in him but also suffer for his sake . . . .

---

[2] Regarding verse 10: ". . . this verse is best understood as a second purpose clause introduced. . . by *'that I may know.'* This construction parallels the . . . clause ['that I may. . .'] that begins at the end of verse 8 and continues through verse 9. . . . This verse should probably be viewed as an expansion of the earlier phrase in verse 8, 'the incomparable value of knowing Christ Jesus my Lord'. . . . Paul appears to define *knowing Christ* as the believers' experiencing of Christ's own death and resurrection" (Silva, *Philippians*, 163).

[3] Paul doesn't mention love in Philippians 3, but as we will see in *Unit 2: Reshaped by the Gospel*, which focuses on Philippians 2, for Paul, love is one of the primary applications of the J-Curve.

5. How does Philippians 1:29 anticipate Philippians 3:9-11? What are the parallels?

6. Let's give a title to each of these two ways of knowing Christ.

Life of Kayla => Life of Christ.

A New Life => New Way of Living.

7. How might Kayla know Jesus differently than she might have in the past?

8. As important as it is to be discipled, read the Bible, attend church, and pray—what are the limitations of those ways of knowing Christ?

9. Think of some analogies from real life of the difference between knowing Jesus by faith and entering into his life. It is the difference between . . . .

- babysitting and _____
- boot camp and _____
- business school and _____
- falling in love and _____

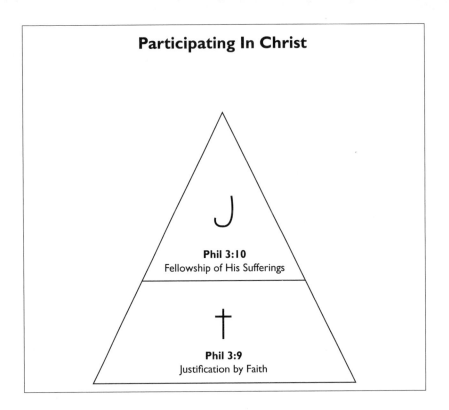

Knowing Jesus with Two Eyes:

JUSTIFICATION BY FAITH	FELLOWSHIP OF HIS SUFFERING & POWER OF HIS RESURRECTION
Symbol: Cross	Symbol: J-Curve
His suffering, not ours.	Our suffering, not his.
Believe the Gospel	Become like the Gospel
Know him by faith, by resting.	Know him by love, by doing.

Saves us from our sins.	Doesn't save us from our sins.
His story transforms my story.	His story becomes my story.
Christ died for me.	I die for you.
A new life.	A living out of the new life.
Deals with pride in principle.	Deals with pride in practice.

10. What is the danger of merging these two ways of knowing Jesus?

11. What is the danger of separating these two ways of knowing Jesus?

12. By putting these two sections parallel to one another, what is Paul suggesting?

Gospel Connection: Two Ways of Knowing

- Like the two natures of Christ, his divinity and his humanity, these two ways of participating in Christ must:
  1. Never be separated.
  2. Never be merged.
  3. Never be reversed.

- For Paul, this is a single act of knowing. For Paul, to believe the gospel necessarily led to entering into Jesus' dying and resurrection life.
- The J-Curve is not application, but a participation in the story of Jesus, a different way of knowing Christ. Calling it application marginalizes a "fellowship of his suffering."

13. What is the danger of a foundation of *justification by faith* not joined with a *fellowship of suffering*?

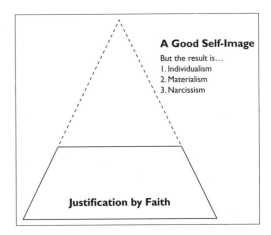

A Good Self-Image
But the result is...
1. Individualism
2. Materialism
3. Narcissism

Justification by Faith

14. What is the danger of a *fellowship of suffering* without *justification by faith*?

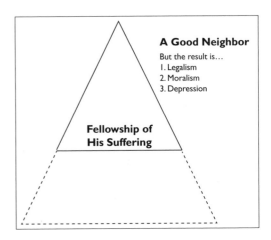

A Good Neighbor
But the result is...
1. Legalism
2. Moralism
3. Depression

Fellowship of His Suffering

If We Isolate Justification by Faith from a Fellowship of His Suffering

"JUSTIFICATION BY FAITH" *Without a Fellowship of His Suffering*	"FELLOWSHIP OF HIS SUFFERING" *Without Justification by Faith*
Jesus is distant. Just need him for salvation.	Jesus is distant. "Dark night of the soul."
Avoids suffering because it has Jesus.	Hunts for suffering to find Jesus.
Wants to feel good, to protect the self.	Wants to experience suffering to get rid of self.
Avoids the J-Curve.	Stuck at the bottom of the J-Curve.
Pride cultivated.	Pride in humility.

Martin Luther wrote referring to justification by faith:

The church is founded on, and consists in, this doctrine alone . . . .[4]

15. Having read Philippians 3:7-11, is Luther correct? What is good about what Luther says? What is incorrect?

Church History: Is Jesus our Mediator or Example? Yes.

Scholar Richard Gaffin, "Too much of our church history . . . has gotten trapped in a false dilemma between Atonement (Christ as Mediator) and conformity (Christ as example). Risking a generalization . . . it does seem fair to say that the churches of the Reformation have shown a much better grasp of the 'for us' of Christ's cross and the gospel [the work of Jesus] than they have of the 'with him' of that gospel, particularly suffering with him [the example of Jesus] . . . . There are few truths which the church down through its history has been more inclined to evade; there are few truths which the church can less afford to evade."[5]

16. Why is this a critical truth for the church to embrace?

---

[4] Luther, *Galatians, xxi.*

[5] Gaffin, "The Usefulness of the Cross," 244.

I BELIEVE THE GOSPEL	I BECOME LIKE THE GOSPEL
FAITH	**LOVE**
Christ dies for me. (message)	I die for you. (method)
JESUS TAKES MY PLACE	**I TAKE YOUR PLACE**
Christ took my burdens at the cross. My weight becomes his.	I take your burdens on. Your weight becomes mine.
He loves me without limit and makes me free, drawing me into close fellowship.	I love without limit and give you freedom, drawing you close to me and God.
JUSTIFICATION BY FAITH	**INCARNATIONAL LOVE**
SONSHIP	**ONENESS**
1. Christ looks. 2. Christ feels. 3. Christ takes the burden. 4. Christ dies, I live. 5. Christ lives a new life.	1. I look. 2. I feel. 3. I take your burden. 4. I die, you live. 5. I live a new life.
• Power to make me right with God is <u>only</u> here. • Always begin with faith & return to faith.	• No power to make me right with God. • Never separate love from faith. • Never mix faith & love.
…Jesus' work becomes more vivid.	As you participate in Jesus' life…

LESSON 10 APPLICATION

Reflect on Believing and Becoming Like the Gospel

1. Why is it helpful to see that following Jesus means both believing the gospel and becoming like the gospel?

1 Peter 2:21-24

[21] For to this you have been called, because Christ also suffered for you, leaving you an example, so that you might follow in his steps. [22] He committed no sin, neither was deceit found in his mouth. [23] When he was reviled, he did not revile in return; when he suffered, he did not threaten, but continued entrusting himself to him who judges justly. [24] He himself bore our sins in his body on the tree, that we might die to sin and live to righteousness. By his wounds you have been healed.

2. How well-balanced is this passage on believing the gospel and becoming like the gospel?

3. Which verse here focuses on "believing the gospel"?

4. Which verses here focus on "becoming like the gospel"?

Scholar Richard Gaffin on 1 Peter 2:21-24

"The requisite balance is nowhere more decisively and effectively struck than in 1 Peter 2:21-25. . . . Peter tells us, 'Christ himself bore our sins in his body on the cross' and 'by his wounds you have been healed. . . .' At the same time, however, Peter is intent on showing that a purpose . . . of Christ's suffering and death is that 'we might die to sin and live for righteousness' and to leave you an example for you to follow in his footsteps. And these footsteps lead, as Paul tells us, into 'the fellowship of his sufferings' and 'being conformed to his death' (Phil. 3:10)."[6]

---

[6] Gaffin, "The Usefulness of the Cross," 243.

5. What is the danger if you ignore justification by faith?

6. What is the danger if you ignore a fellowship of his sufferings?

7. Which "eye" have you been better at seeing Jesus with—the eye of justification by faith or the eye of a fellowship of his sufferings? How has that shaped your life?

8. What is one insight you've had from your study today that you'd like to hang onto in the week to come?

LESSON 11: IN SPORTS

SECTION 1: In Field Hockey

Philippians 3:3-11

[3] For we are "the circumcision," who worship by the Spirit of God and *boast* in Christ Jesus and not in the flesh putting confidence—[4] though I myself have reason for confidence in the flesh also. If anyone else thinks he has reason for confidence in the flesh, I have more:

[5] circumcised on the eighth day,
    of the people of Israel,
        of the tribe of Benjamin,
            a Hebrew of Hebrews;
as to the law, a Pharisee;
    [6] as to zeal, a persecutor of the church;
        as to righteousness under the law, blameless.

[7] But whatever gain I had, I counted as loss for the sake of Christ. [8] Indeed, I count everything as loss because of the surpassing worth of knowing Christ Jesus my Lord. For his sake I have suffered the loss of all things and count them as rubbish, in order that I may gain Christ [9] and be found in him, not having a righteousness of my own that comes from the law, but that which comes through faith in Christ, the righteousness from God that depends on faith—[10] that I may know him and the power of his resurrection, and the fellowship of his suffering, taking the form of his death, [11] that by any means possible I may attain the resurrection from the dead.

Personal Illustration: In Sports

I loved watching my daughter Emily play field hockey in high school. I know the sport well because I watched three of my sisters and then Emily's sister, Ashley, play it. For those of you not familiar with field hockey, it is like ice hockey except played on a field like soccer. I know the rules so I can usually see when refs miss calls. I've even had one coach remind me that she was the coach, not I!

One season Emily and her friend were benched for a good share of the season. Many thought they were benched because they weren't the coach's favorites. Neither Emily nor I enjoyed this. I asked Emily if she wanted me to talk to the coach, but she said, "No, I'll do it, Dad." I was thankful for her maturity.

I ran into another parent at the gym during all this, and she said, "I can't believe what the coach is doing with Emily and her friend." I said, "I'm actually thankful that Emily has this low-level suffering on my watch. Life is much more like sitting on the bench than starring in a game." I can still see the shock on this mom's face. We were both believers, but she was "in sports" and I was "in Christ." That is, her esteem, what she valued, came from her children and how well they did in sports. So the defense of her kids in sports was critical. On the other hand, I was in Jesus so when Emily encountered suffering, I was bummed, but thankful for an opportunity for her to be drawn into Jesus. Even though our kids were doing exactly the same thing—playing sports—we inhabited different worlds. My "in-Jesus" perspective shaped my response to Emily's hardship. Being "in Christ" took the steam out of me because my passion was for Emily to be "in Christ."

1. Is sports the problem?

2. How is faith critical to watching your child unjustly sitting on a bench?

3. Read 3:9. How would the mom complete the phrase "a righteousness of my own that comes from _____"?

4. How would Paul Miller complete the phrase "a righteousness of my own that comes from _____"?

5. Are there areas in your life where you would be tempted to be like this mom? How would you complete the phrase "a righteousness of my own that comes from _____"?

6. What about justice for Emily? What about confronting the coach?

SECTION 2: The J-Curve on the Bench

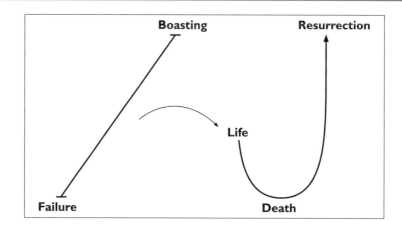

7. Reread 3:7-8. Which of these two charts is Paul Miller's loss? Which is his gain?

8. If your righteousness comes from sports, what is your attitude towards the J-Curve suffering of your daughter sitting on the bench?

9. Let's say Paul Miller's wife disagreed with his not going to the coach. How does that change the J-Curve for Paul?

10. If living in the J-Curve is your life goal, how does that reshape your vision of life?

Two Options When Confronted with a Fellowship of His Suffering

Option 1: Suffering + *self-will* =

Option 2: Suffering + *surrender* =

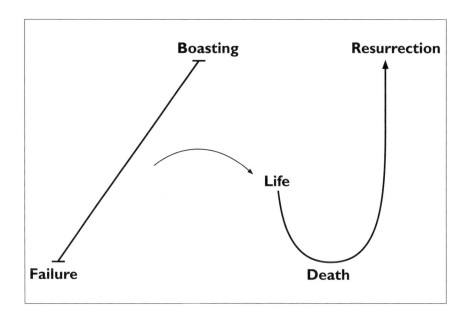

LESSON 11 APPLICATION

Reflect on Field Hockey Story

1. If Emily were your daughter, how would you have handled her being benched?

2. What principles or thoughts would have guided your interactions?

3. Do you have a specific story in your life similar to this? How did you handle it?

4. How would embracing a "fellowship of his sufferings" have transformed your story?

Reflect on "In Sports"

5. Think of this Field Hockey-Mom. Imagine what she might say about her daughter playing field hockey.

   Boasts. . .

   a)

b)

c)

Complaints. . .
   a)

   b)

   c)

A "boast" can be either positive ("I keep a clean house") or negative ("Look how heavy she is"). They can either be earned ("I did this") or unearned ("I am an American").
   Some examples:
      "I would never let my kids behave like that."
      "Look how they keep their lawn."
      "Her house is a mess. She is just lazy."
      "I bet I make three times what he makes."

6. **How do you know if you are enjoying sports or "in sports"? What is the difference?**

7. **The story of Emily is also a story of a perceived injustice. How did Paul Miller combine a concern for justice with not being "in sports"?**

8. What red flags might alert you to the problem of being "in sports"? Remember, participating in sports, like circumcision, is not wrong. It just can't give life!

Examples: 1) Rushing by people might be a red flag that I'm prizing my work or my time more than love. 2) Anger might be a red flag that someone has taken something away from me that is a source of life.

Reflect on Not Boasting (Lesson 2, Section 3)

9. If you'd not been thanked or given credit for an idea, how would you have handled it?

10. What principles or thoughts would have guided your interactions?

11. Do you have a specific story in your life similar to this—a story where you were overlooked or not thanked? How did you handle it?

12. Would the outcome have been different if you had embraced a fellowship of his sufferings? How?

13. What is one insight you've had from your study today that you'd like to hang onto in the week to come?

LESSON 12: A DAY IN THE LIFE OF RANDY AND SALLY

A Day in the Life of Randy and Sally[1]

Philippians 3:7-11

[7] But whatever gain I had, I counted as loss for the sake of Christ. [8] Indeed, I count everything as loss because of the surpassing worth of knowing Christ Jesus my Lord. For his sake I have suffered the loss of all things and count them as rubbish, in order that I may gain Christ [9] and be found in him, not having a righteousness of my own that comes from the law, but that which comes through faith in Christ, the righteousness from God that depends on faith—[10] that I may know him and the power of his resurrection, and the fellowship of his suffering, taking the form of his death, [11] that by any means possible I may attain the resurrection from the dead.

8:00 a.m. – Car Won't Start

Randy: I'm a pastor of a church in Virginia. I just got back from a West Coast trip, so I felt some pressure to get into work. I had a lesson to prepare for that evening, plus a lunch appointment. Wouldn't you know it, but Sally's car wouldn't start. It is a diesel and we've been having trouble with it, especially when it is cold outside . . . and this was winter. I delayed getting in to work to jump-start it and get it to the garage.

Sally: I couldn't believe it when the car didn't start. For weeks now, we've had problems with our battery. And it's worse in winter. He knows this. I've reminded him about this several times, but he keeps putting it off. I lost the first two hours of my day because he hadn't taken the time to get a new battery. This should have been fixed weeks ago.

---

[1] Names have been changed.

4:00 p.m. – Calls Wife

Randy: I got into work about ten o'clock, two hours late, so I barely dented my in-basket. During lunch, I lost track of time, partly because I had not changed my watch from West Coast time, so I thought I still had time! When I got back to the office at 2:30, I only had one and a half hours to get the lesson done for our small group that night. Because I have so many evening meetings, I try to get home by 4:00 to take pressure off Sally. I called her at four and asked her if I could come home at five. I thought it only fair since I'd helped her out this morning.

Sally: When he called me at 4:00 to ask for more time, I said okay, but I was frustrated. Now I had all the pressure of our kids' homework while trying to make dinner, plus we had small group tonight, so we had to be out on time. He messed up the beginning and the end of my day.

5:30 p.m. – Rushes through Dinner

Randy: I got home about 5:30 in the middle of dinner.

Sally: Dinner was rushed. I can't think of how many times this has happened. Why do his problems become my problems?

7:00 p.m. – Multitasks with Kids

Randy: After dinner I helped get the kids ready for bedtime. I still wasn't finished with the lesson, so in between helping them, I reviewed the lesson. In the middle of this, Sally came upstairs, saw me working on the lesson, and blew up. It was not a happy moment. I don't think Sally appreciated how pressured my day was. She seemed to have forgotten that I'd helped her out that morning, and that had impacted my whole day.

Sally: I went upstairs after dinner to check on the kids, and I found him sneaking in his lesson preparation for our small group time instead of helping the kids. I'm sorry, but I blew. He's not only neglecting me, but now the kids as well. He had it coming. Augh!

ACT 1: 8:00 a.m. – Car Won't Start

1. What is Randy's "goodness," from Randy's point of view?

2. What is Sally's view of Randy when he fixes the car?

3. What makes self-righteousness hard to see for both Randy and Sally?

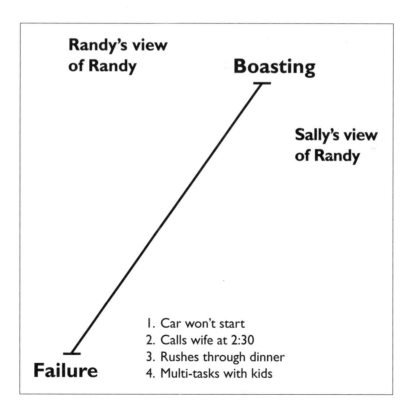

4. We've said early in this study "all of life is gift." In this situation, what is Randy and Sally's summary of life?

Theological Background: Karma or Charis

Randy and Sally, in this specific situation, are both acting like Hindus. Hinduism believes in karma—we are always being rewarded for our past behavior. If you have had a good past life, then you build up good karma and come back as a higher form of life. If you are bad, then you accumulate bad karma. We are all instinctive Hindus.

Instead of *karma*, Randy and Sally could embrace *charis* (Greek for grace). If you receive grace, then you extend grace. When we extend grace, we are touching the deepest structure of the universe. Trees, grass, stars, air, our very existence . . . all of life is a gift. Our response to gift is wonder and thanksgiving. And thus the Flesh's first response to life with us at the center is thanklessness (Romans 1:21).[2]

5. Randy knows and loves the doctrine of justification by faith. What is Randy failing to do with the doctrine?

6. How does the J-Curve (Phil. 3:10-11) help Randy receive Sally's criticism?

---

[2] Charles Malik's *The Wonder of Being* (Word Books, 1974) first taught me that "all of life is gift" when I read it during college. Malik was an Orthodox believer, a philosopher and statesman from Lebanon.

7. If Sally reflects on her justification by faith, how might that change her response?

8. If Sally is forgiving and gentle, what risk does she face with Randy?

9. If Randy doesn't realize he's messed up her day, what is going to happen to her life? How will she feel?

10. If she welcomes Randy's "gift," how will that create a "fellowship of his suffering"?

ACT 2: 4:00 p.m. – Calls Wife

11. What is Randy's view of Randy at 4 p.m.?

12. What is Sally's view of Randy after this phone call?

13. If Randy wasn't "earning points" but simply loving his wife when he fixed the car, how would that change his attitude towards his wife at 4 p.m.?

14. How does the J-Curve apply to Randy apologizing to Sally here?

15. If Sally was less self-righteous (giving Randy a bad grade), how would that change her response?

16. How does the J-Curve apply to Sally? What risks does she face by being kind?

ACT 3: 5:30 p.m. – Rushes through Dinner

17. What is Randy's view of Randy?

18. What might an in-Christ Randy say when he comes in late?

19. If Sally is in Christ, what might be her response to Randy's repeated failures?

20. What does faith look like for Sally when Randy keeps messing up? How does she handle her heart?

Sally must constantly cry out for grace. Only if she sees that her critical, judgmental heart is as bad as Randy's disorganized, excuse-making heart will she enter into the world of grace. She must be constant in prayer. Her first battle is with her heart, not Randy. If, by the Spirit, she wins the battle with her heart, she will win the battle with Randy. She can receive his disorganization as from the Lord, as a fellowship of his sufferings.

ACT 4: 7:00 p.m. – Multitasks with Kids

21. What suffering is Randy avoiding by multitasking?

22. How could realizing he is in a "fellowship of his suffering" change Randy?

⊘ **Gospel Connection: Randy's Heart**

Randy must cry out for grace when Sally blows up at him. Only if he is grounded in Christ will he be able to look past Sally's anger and look at her real concerns. He will have to fight the desire to see himself as a victim. His first battle is with his heart.

He needs the Spirit to help him see how his disorganization affects Sally.

23. What might be a better response for Sally?

24. What suffering might Sally be avoiding by blowing up at Randy? What will it feel like if she doesn't?

Gospel Connection: Allergic to the J-Curve

Randy and Sally are both allergic to the J-Curve. They spent their whole day avoiding suffering. Sally avoids the suffering of a disorganized husband by nursing her victim story. Randy avoids the suffering of facing an angry wife by not apologizing.

LESSON 12 APPLICATION

Reflect on Randy and Sally

1. Are you more like Randy or Sally?

2. Write out your own "Randy" or "Sally" story. Describe the story in detail. Try to come up with a specific incident, not a list of generalities. It is okay to disguise names and location. Here are some clues to help you come up with a story:
   - When was the last time you were angry? Do you have anyone who has mistreated you?
   - Do you have a difficult relationship at home, with relatives or neighbors, or at work?
   - When did someone embarrass you?

Reflect on Justification by Faith

3. You can answer this positively, negatively, or both ways.
   - Negative: Can you describe any self-righteousness on your part in your story?
   - Positive: Can you describe any victory over self-righteousness?

4. Rephrase Paul's statement, "A righteousness of my own that comes from the law," for you in your story.
   "A righteousness of my own that comes from _____."

Reflect on a Fellowship of His Suffering

5. You can answer this positively, negatively, or both ways.
   - Was there any suffering that you avoided in your story?
   - Was there any suffering you received?

6. If you had been reflecting on the "fellowship of his suffering" that Jesus invites us into, how might that have changed you in the story?

Look Ahead

7. How might resting in God's justification of you by faith in Jesus help you this week?

8. How might reflecting on the "fellowship of his suffering" change your attitude towards suffering this week?

9. What is one insight you've had from your study today that you'd like to hang onto in the week to come?

LESSON 13: A JESUS JOURNEY

Philippians 3:9-21

. . . that I may gain Christ [9] and be found in him, not having a righteousness of my own that comes from the law, but that which comes through faith in Christ, the righteousness from God that depends on faith—

[10] that I may know him and the power of his resurrection, and the fellowship of his suffering, taking the form of his death, [11] that by any means possible I may attain the resurrection from the dead.

[12] Not that I have already obtained this or am already perfect, but I press on to make it my own, because Christ Jesus has made me his own. [13] Brothers, I do not consider that I have made it my own. But one thing I do: forgetting what lies behind and straining forward to what lies ahead, [14] I press on toward the goal for the prize of the upward call of God in Christ Jesus. [15] Let those of us who are mature think this way, and if in anything you think otherwise, God will reveal that also to you. [16] Only let us hold true to what we have attained.

[17] Brothers, join in imitating me, and keep your eyes on those who walk according to the example you have in us. [18] For many, of whom I have often told you and now tell you even with tears, walk as enemies of the cross of Christ. [19] Their end is destruction, their god is their belly, and they glory in their shame, with minds set on earthly things. [20] But our citizenship is in heaven, and from it we await a Savior, the Lord Jesus Christ, [21] who will transform our lowly body to be like his glorious body, by the power that enables him even to subject all things to himself.

1. What metaphor or picture from the Greek world does Paul use in 3:12-14?

2. What makes a race or marathon a good metaphor for the Christian life?

3. What is the goal of Paul's marathon? Hint: see verses 20-21.

4. What false, alternative race does Paul describe?

5. What else is Paul doing in 3:10-11 that is critical for a good journey?

Summary: The Jesus-Journey

For their Jesus-Journey, Paul offers the Philippians a:

- Map—the pattern of Jesus dying and rising.
- Guide—Paul himself as one who embodies Jesus' pattern of dying and rising.
- Goal—the resurrection.
- Perspective (my location)—we aren't there yet—"already, not yet."
- Warnings—don't follow people who are on bad journeys.

SECTION 2: "Forgetting What Lies Behind"

6. When Paul says, "forgetting what lies behind," what is he forgetting?

7. The pre-Christian Paul imprisoned and murdered Christians. What is remarkable about how Paul handles his past? How do we tend to handle the past?[1]

8. How does justification by faith free Paul from being trapped in his past failures?

9. How does the "fellowship of his sufferings" free Paul from being trapped by bitterness (by other people's sins)?

(◎) **Gospel Connection: Freed from the Past**

Paul's discovery of Jesus transformed how he looked at his past. Paul is totally free from the burden of guilt (his sin) or bitterness (others' sin).

(⌢) **Modern Culture: Trapped by the Past**

At times, it can be helpful to look at our past. The Old Testament looks at Israel's past, and we learn from it. Modern psychology teaches that understanding the past frees us in the present. It can produce some change, but like all "law," it is powerless to change the heart. In fact, many people get trapped by looking at their past, thinking that their past controls them in the present. The past can be toxic because hurt dwelt on can feed bitterness. Focusing on the past can further entangle us in ourselves rather than freeing us.[2]

10. What new story shapes how Paul looks at his past?

11. What else is Paul focused on that keeps him from getting entangled in the past?

SECTION 3: "Already, Not Yet"

12. Where is Paul himself on this journey? Has Paul reached the end?

---

[1]   Acts 8:3; 9:1, 2, 13, 21; 22:4; 26:10.

[2]   "Our modern rejection of God makes us disoriented. The mind is self-entangled in itself and is not sure it really knows what it thinks it knows" (Malik, *The Wonder of Being*, 30). See also 46, 70. Malik is an Eastern Orthodox philosopher who saved my faith during college.

A key to understanding Paul the apostle is the phrase, "Already, Not Yet." By *faith* we are *already* united with Christ in his death and resurrection, but at the same time we are still waiting in *hope* for the final resurrection. So we are *already* dead to sin, but we are *not yet* dead to sin, we are still fighting it. "Already" looks at the past by faith "Not yet" looks to the future in hope.

13. How do you see both "already" and "not yet" in 3:13?

14. How does "already, not yet" help us understand Paul being declared righteous in verse 9?

SECTION 4: Right Now! = J-Curve

15. If "already" refers to the past and "not yet" to the future, what is missing?

We can expand our slogan to include the *present* by saying . . .

"Already, Not Yet . . . Right Now!"

---

[3] "Already, not yet" was popularized by George Eldon Ladd, but it came originally from Geerhardus Vos, the Princeton scholar. The "already" is actually the future invading the past and the present.

	JESUS' DEATH AND RESURRECTION	PHRASE
Past	Jesus' death for us is finished. Because we are in Jesus and have already died with him, our sins are **already** paid for. We have already been declared righteous. Already, *by faith*, we have died with Christ and are raised with him.	"Already"
Future	We look forward to the future resurrection when our new bodies will match our new hearts. We've **not yet** received this. But we taste the future resurrection **now** by the Spirit's presence in our lives.	"Not Yet"
Present	We reenact Jesus' death and resurrection **right now** in the present. That is the pattern of our lives between Jesus' past resurrection and our future resurrection. The work of *love* ("right now!") makes the work of *faith* ("already") real. *Love* makes *faith* present.	"Right Now!"

ALREADY	NOT YET	RIGHT NOW!
Past	Future	Present
The work of faith.	The work of hope.	The work of love.
Justification.	Glorification.	Sanctification.
Declared righteous.	Completely righteous.	Becoming righteous.
Being—who I am.	What I will be.	Becoming—who I am becoming.
Participation.	Perfection.	Practice.
United with Christ in his death and resurrection by faith.	Resurrected bodies! No more death.	Dying and rising with Christ on a daily basis as I love.
Already sons and daughters of God because of Jesus' death and resurrection.	Fully, completely a son or daughter of God, in his presence, fully transformed.	Becoming sons and daughters by learning to pray, obey, believe.

Theological Insight: Analogy to Already, Not Yet, Right Now!

Imagine you are an American soldier in a landing craft approaching the beach at Normandy for the invasion of France on D-Day, June 6, 1944. What are your thoughts?

- **"Already."**

- "Not Yet."

- "Right Now!"

Philippians 3:8-21

. . . that I may gain Christ [9] and be found in him, not having a righteousness of my own that comes from the law, but that which comes through faith in Christ, the righteousness from God that depends on faith = MY **PAST** IS NOW RADICALLY RESHAPED. BY FAITH IN CHRIST, I AM COUNTED RIGHTEOUS. THAT STOPS ME FROM STRIVING IN THE PRESENT TO CREATE MY OWN RIGHTEOUSNESS.

— [10] that I may know him and the power of his resurrection, and the fellowship of his suffering, taking the form of his death, [11] that by any means possible I may attain the resurrection from the dead. = MY **PRESENT** IS BEING RESHAPED BY JESUS' **PAST** STORY. HE PROVIDES THE NEW MAP OF MY LIFE.

[12] Not that I have already obtained this or am already perfect, but I press on to make it my own, because Christ Jesus has made me his own. = I'M NOT IN THE **FUTURE** YET. I LIVE BETWEEN JESUS' **PAST** DEATH AND RESURRECTION AND MY **FUTURE** RESURRECTION. [13] Brothers, I do not consider that I have made it my own. But one thing I do: forgetting what lies behind and straining forward to what lies ahead, [14] I press on toward the goal for the prize of the upward call of God in Christ Jesus. = FOCUSING ON THE **FUTURE** RESURECTION GIVES ME ZEAL FOR THE **PRESENT**. [15] Let those of us who are mature think this way, and if in anything you think otherwise, God will reveal that also to you. [16] Only let us hold true to what we have attained.

[17] Brothers, join in imitating me, and keep your eyes on those who walk according to the example you have in us. [18] For many, of whom I have often told you and now tell you even with tears, walk as enemies of the cross of Christ. [19] Their end is destruction, their god is their belly, and they glory in their shame, with minds set on earthly things. = THESE PEOPLE LIVE ONLY FOR THEIR **PRESENT** PLEASURE. NO MASTER GOAL, MAP, OR GUIDE SHAPES THEIR LIVES OTHER THAN SELF AND PLEASURE. THEY ARE ON A SAD JOURNEY TO DEATH. [20] But our citizenship is in heaven, and from it we await a Savior, the Lord Jesus Christ, [21] who will transform our lowly body to be like his glorious body, by the power that enables him even to subject all things to himself. = I CAN'T WAIT FOR THE **FUTURE** WHEN JESUS COMES BACK AND RESURRECTS ALL OF US, GIVING US NEW BODIES THAT FIT OUR NEW HEARTS! THE **FUTURE** GIVES ME HOPE IN THE **PRESENT**.

16. How does this help us think of our lives as Christians?

LESSON 13 APPLICATION

Reflect on Life as a Race

1. How have you seen your life as a journey led by the spirit of Jesus? What has your journey been like? What kind of a pilgrim are you?

2. Are there events in your past where you feel trapped by your failures or sin or by other people's sins against you?

3. What do you think about the idea that the old you—including all your past failures and even other people's sins against you—died with Jesus at the cross?

4. So when thoughts come up of your past failures, where do you take them?

5. How does focusing on the future resurrection reshape how you think of the present?

Reflect on "Already, Not Yet"

6. How does "Already, Not Yet" describe you as you fight against sin? Think of your battle with a particular sin.

7. How does "Already, Not Yet" encourage you?

8. How is it helpful to add "Right Now!"?

Reflect on "Already, Not Yet, Right Now!"

9. How is pregnancy like "Already, Not Yet, Right Now!"? Explain each of the three categories.

   Already

   Not Yet

   Right Now!

10. How is being a teenager like "Already, Not Yet, Right Now!"?

   Already

   Not Yet

   Right Now!

11. Reflect on a particular sin and show how it maps on "Already, Not Yet, Right Now!" For example: gossip, harshness, laziness. The example of overeating below is to help you.

Already. . . I've died to the sin of overeating. I died with Jesus.

_____

Not Yet . . . I'll likely struggle with the temptation to overeat all my life. One day, at Jesus' return, I will finally be rid of my Flesh.

_____

Right Now! . . . Right now, the Spirit can give me the grace to put to death this temptation of overeating. I work at not feeding my temptation by throwing out all the candy in the house!

_____

LESSON 14: LIVE IT UP OR TOUGH IT OUT?

SECTION 1: The World of Pleasure: Epicureans

Philippians 3:17-21

> [17] Brothers, join in imitating me, and keep your eyes on those who walk according to the example you have in us. [18] For many, of whom I have often told you and now tell you even with tears, walk as enemies of the cross of Christ. [19] Their end is destruction, their god is their belly, and they glory in their shame, with minds set on earthly things. [20] But our citizenship is in heaven, and from it we await a Savior, the Lord Jesus Christ, [21] who will transform our lowly body to be like his glorious body, by the power that enables him even to subject all things to himself.

1. What is the mindset of these opponents of the gospel in verses 18 and 19?

🕐 Historical Background: Epicureans

This is almost a perfect description of Epicureans. In the Greco-Roman world, Epicureans lived for pleasure. They asked, "Is this good for me?" Their motto was, "Eat, drink, and be merry, for tomorrow we die."[1]

---

[1] We don't know for sure if Paul's opponents were Epicureans. Some scholars (N. T. Wright, and F. Hawthorne and Ralph P. Martin) hold that these are Judaizers. I am persuaded by the strong similarity with Epicureanism. At one level it is a moot point, because Epicureanism and Stoicism are the two polar drifts of the human heart outside of Jesus. They are immortalized in Jesus' parable of the Prodigal Son. The older brother is a Stoic and the younger, an Epicurean. See Thielman, *The NIV Application Commentary: Philippians*, 198. For a good summary of Stoics and Epicureans see Wright, *Paul and the Faithfulness of God*, 211-229.

2. How is this different from Paul implying that Christians are on a journey?

3. What does it likely mean when Paul says they "glory in their shame"?

4. How does Paul respond to the Epicurean mindset in Phil. 3:17-21?

5. How is Paul going after the Epicurean mindset in "the power of his resurrection and the fellowship of sharing in his sufferings"?

6. How do we see the Epicurean mindset in our culture?

Historical Background: Stoics and Epicureans

In the Greco-Roman world, the opposite of the Epicureans were the Stoics. Stoics had high principles and lived for duty and honor. They asked, "Is this good? Am I in harmony with the *logos*, the 'word' or mind behind the universe?" But their morality was empty. They worked at having a balanced, passionless life that avoided extremes. So a Stoic endured suffering because it developed character. An Epicurean avoided suffering because it was painful to the self. Both centered on self.[2]

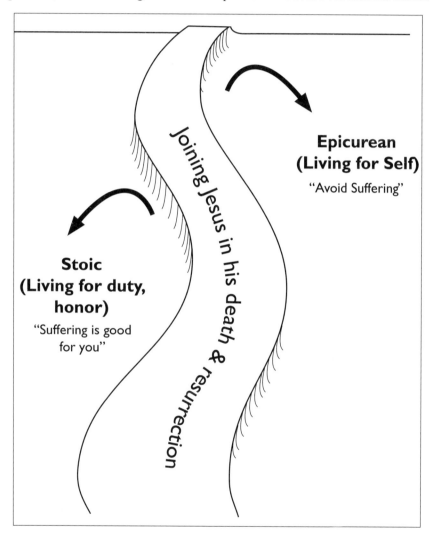

---

[2] While these patterns of Stoics and Epicureans are generally true, I am simplifying a relatively complex world for the sake of clarity. For a more technical summary of Stoics and Epicureans see N. T. Wright's book, *Paul and the Faithfulness of God*, 211-228.

Summary Chart:

STOICISM	EPICUREANISM
"No pain, no gain."	"No pain, only pleasure."
"What is the logos, the pattern of the universe that I can conform to?"	"What is best for me?"
Law without meaning or purpose.	Lawless.
Embraces suffering.	Avoids suffering.
God is their mind.	God is their belly.
Living for duty, honor.	Living for self.
Asceticism.	Hedonism.
Doesn't know how to abound.	Doesn't know how to abase.
Stuck at the bottom of the J-Curve.	Avoids the bottom of the J-Curve.
Needs justification by faith.	Needs a fellowship of his suffering.

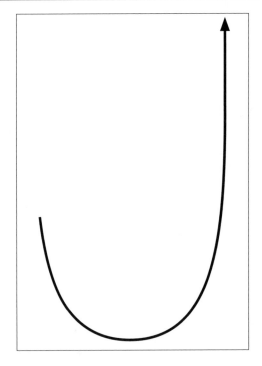

Philippians 4:12-13

> [12] I know how to be brought low, and I know how to abound. In any and every circumstance, I have learned the secret of facing plenty and hunger, abundance and need. [13] I can do all things through him who strengthens me.

7. What is Paul's secret of facing plenty and hunger, abundance and need?

⊘ Gospel Connection: How the Gospel Answers Stoics and Epicureans

Believing the Gospel: A Stoic, like the Pharisee in the parable of the Pharisee and the tax collector, creates his own righteousness by conforming to the "mind" of the universe. He works at doing the right thing. The gospel asks the Stoic to surrender his pride, realize that he can't even live up to his own rules, and receive by faith the righteousness that comes from being in Christ. The Epicurean doesn't care about doing the right thing. He lives for his own pleasure. The gospel asks him to surrender his will and come follow Jesus.

Becoming Like the Gospel: An Epicurean pushes suffering away, while a Stoic embraces suffering because it makes him a better person. Unlike the Stoic, the Christian in the face of suffering turns to Christ. We embrace Christ – not the suffering itself. We don't seek opportunities to suffer. Life brings them to us. In fact, Christians should flee suffering (a tornado is coming), anticipate suffering (insurance, medical checkups), or soften its effect (medical care, hospitals, etc.). The gospel calls the Stoic-like person to not get stuck in death but look for resurrection now and at Jesus' second coming.

Unlike the Epicurean, the Christian embraces a fellowship of his sufferings. There is nothing more painful than spending your life running from pain. The gospel calls the Epicurean-like person not to grasp at resurrection but receive the present fellowship of his sufferings.

Summary: All of us need to both believe the gospel and become like the gospel. Some of us need to emphasize believing more, while others need to emphasize becoming like the gospel more.

LESSON 14 APPLICATION

1. Are you more of an Epicurean or a Stoic? Explain.

Reflect on Epicureans

2. Do you know people who are Epicureans? Describe one of them.

3. What happens to the Epicurean's heart over time?

4. What happens to an Epicurean's relationships over time?

5. In what ways are you tempted to be an Epicurean? Describe what that looks like in your life.

6. How does the gospel (past, present, and future) help you not be an Epicurean?

Reflect on Stoics

7. Do you know people who are Stoics—good people, living for duty but who have no meaning in their life? Describe one of them.

8. What happens to the Stoic's heart over time?

9. What happens to a Stoic's relationships over time?

10. In what ways are you a Stoic? Describe what that looks like in your life.

11. How does the gospel (past, present, and future) help you not be a Stoic?

Stoic and Epicurean Reactions

12. Recall the Kayla story from Lesson 9. If Kayla was a Stoic, how would she react? If Kayla was an Epicurean, how would she react?

13. Recall the Emily hockey story from Lesson 11. If Paul Miller was a Stoic, how would he react? If Paul Miller was an Epicurean, how would he react?

ACKNOWLEDGMENTS

I've benefited from the hard work of many scholars, but these scholars in particular have been an immense help to me: Anthony Thiselton (1 Corinthians), Richard Gaffin (insights on the gospel), Simon Gathercole (the theme of boasting), Peter O'Brien (Philippians), Michael Gorman (study of cruciformity), Robert Tannehill (insights on boasting), and Peter Brown (understanding the Greek and Roman mind).

I'm also thankful for the many churches that participated in the J-Curve Seminar, giving me enormously helpful feedback: West End Presbyterian Church (Richmond, VA), Chelten Church (Philadelphia, PA), Westlake Church (Lusanne, Switzerland), Trinity Presbyterian Church (Lakeland, FL), Redeemer City Church (Winter Haven, FL), Redemption Church (Phoenix, AZ) and New Life Presbyterian Church (Glenside, PA). My son, John Miller, and Rich Cannon both independently encouraged me to use the title "J-Curve."

Behind the scenes, I'm especially thankful for my friend Timo Strawbridge and his development work that freed me to write. Julie Courtney, as usual, did an excellent job as a developmental editor; Maggie Snyder, our editor-in-training, had many helpful insights; Michele B. Walton handled titling, publicity, marketing, creating templates, and many other tasks as our seeJesus Press Publisher; Liz Voboril, our Director of Communications provided wisdom along the way. A special thanks to our office team (Donna Herr, Dianne Baker, and Shirley Kenney) for providing so much behind the scenes work. The board of seeJesus (Drew Bennett, Nessa Parks, Bob Loker, Steve Young, Blair Simmons, and Dwight Smith) provided wisdom and leadership.

I'm particularly thankful to my wife Jill for encouraging me to "get this done"! And last but not least, my daughter Kim prays for my writing every day!

APPENDIX: REFLECTIONS ON THE NEW PERSPECTIVE

The New Perspective on Paul (NPP) is an influential and increasingly dominant scholarly movement of largely American and English scholars that has "a new perspective" on Paul's theology. More than anything, it critiques the traditional Protestant view of justification by faith that we've inherited from Luther. E. P. Sanders' influential book, Paul and Palestinian Judaism (1977), launched the movement with a fresh reading of Jewish literature written between 200 BC and 200 AD. Sanders argues that no first century Jew thought he was earning his salvation. They already believed they were elect by virtue of their being in the covenant—born as a Jew, circumcised, etc. They kept the law to be faithful to the covenant. Thus, our stereotype of the Pharisees as legalists isn't correct because they weren't trying to work their way into heaven.

Here are some of my positive reactions to NPP.

- NPP scholars pay attention to texts and their cultural context. Thus, they often have thought-provoking readings. I am often challenged in reading them.
- They've forced conservative evangelical scholars to dig deep into Paul and not just retreat into systematic theology (as valuable as systematic theology is).
- NPP scholars (the big three: E. P. Sanders, James Dunn, N. T. Wright) emphasize Paul's Jewish lens. This has helped scholars break free from the "Greek lens" of 19th century liberal German scholars and re-discover Paul's Jewishness. The rediscovery of Jesus and Paul's Jewishness in the last 30 years is a significant break from 200 years of liberal scholarship that has made Jesus, in particular, almost incoherent. The high-water mark of this old liberal perspective is the 1990s Jesus Seminar, a road show for liberal scholarship. N. T. Wright has brilliantly critiqued Jesus Seminar scholar Marcus Borg. The NPP, following Albert Schweitzer, represents a real break with this liberal past. This has been an enormous help to the church.
- With the traditional evangelical focus on individual salvation (psychology of the gospel), the NPP has made us aware of corporate elements of salvation (sociology of the gospel) and the "mind" of late second-century Judaism. They are concerned to help us rediscover Paul's vision of community.
- I share the NPP's concern that we've not grounded our ethic in the gospel. (That's the point of this course.) So Paul's idea of a "fellowship of his suffering" permeates their thinking. For example, see Michael Gorman's *Cruciformity* and N. T. Wright's opening discussing of Philemon in *Paul and the Faithfulness of God.*
- The NPP is not classical liberalism. It handles biblical texts with much more respect. Some evangelical scholars consider themselves NPP. N. T. Wright is a devout believer whose writings have often enlightened and moved me. (E. P. Sanders is a classic liberal Protestant.)

Here is a partial list of my cautions. For a fuller list, see my Lesson Notes below.

- I believe that the NPP's key readings of Paul miss the mark. Luther is at times poorly nuanced and reads justification by faith into texts where it is not present, but in general I think Luther understands Paul on justification. I've tried reading Paul from the viewpoint of the NPP, and it just doesn't hold up. I don't know how Paul could have said more clearly that we are justified by faith. By the time the NPP is finished with the gospel, it is no longer the gospel.
- The NPP defines three key words or phrases differently: *justification*, *faith*, and *works of the law*. *Faith* becomes *faithfulness; works of the law* becomes something merely Jewish, and *justification* becomes something I do. All of these move us in a crypto-Catholic direction and away from free justification.
- The NPP has overreacted to the Reformation bias towards the individual (psychology) and over emphasized "the group" (sociology). It dislikes the simplicity of the gospel that even my daughter Kim, with all her disabilities, can understand.
- Because the NPP comes out of the world of mainstream scholarship it has some of classical liberalism's bias: it is allergic to judgment, the wrath of God, propitiation, or the atonement. So N. T. Wright in *Paul and the Faithfulness of God*, when discussing Paul's view of sin, never mentions God's anger at sin.
- N. T. Wright is currently the most influential and brilliant scholar of the NPP. I read most of what he writes because he approaches texts in such fresh ways, but my general rule for Wright is that he's about 60% brilliant and 40% odd. He's very intuitive and creative, but he often lets that get the better of him.

I've found the biblical studies marked with a double asterisk in the bibliography to be particularly helpful in responding to the NPP. In particular, Lee Iron's dissertation is a careful refutation of NPP's definition of the righteousness as covenant faithfulness.

Lesson Notes

These lesson notes are additional comments on the NPP that relate to specific lessons in 1. United With Christ. We didn't include them in the lesson footnotes because they were so extensive.

1. (Lesson 1, Section 1) The NPP misses how life-legalism dominated 1st century Judaism and for that matter, the human heart. They presume that because most devout Jews had a form of grace and thus seemed assured of their election they weren't legalists. Qumran documents (4QMMT) or any of the gospels confront the reader with both legalism and tribalism.
2. The NPP tends to make the Pharisees "the good guys" (partly out of reaction to the German liberal scholarship's anti-Semitism). For example, when Wright discusses the worldview of the Pharisees (*Paul and the Faithfulness of God,* 184-185), he surveys multiple late 2nd Temple texts but makes no reference to the clear psychological picture of the Pharisees in the Gospels. The NPP minimizes how life-dominating the Jewish boast was. Paul's list of seven boasts is psychological *and* sociological. Paul places himself high in his tribe, which itself is a boast against other tribes.
3. (Lesson 2, Section 2) Paul's language ("the Flesh") suggests he is not merely speaking about a narrow Jewish problem (as the NPP would have us believe), but a problem for all mankind. The NPP over-reads their Jewish lens and misses how Paul repeatedly goes universal (Rom. 1-5) when talking about the human condition.

4. (Lesson 2, Section 1) The phrase "works of the law" only appears in Romans, Galatians and the Dead Sea Scrolls' "Sectarian Manifesto" 4QMMT: 4Q393-399. The Manifesto is an example of legalism's emphasis on outward purity as opposed to Paul's emphasis on the heart and the inability to be pure before God. Thomas Schreiner's article, *"Works of Law" in Paul* in Novum Testamentum XXXIII, 3 (1991), 217-244, is a good summary. See Michael O. Wise, Martin G. Abegg Jr., and Edward M. Cook, *The Dead Sea Scrolls: A New Translation* (New York: HarperCollins, 2005), 454-462.

5. (Lesson 6, Section 4) NPP scholars thought Luther misread Paul and misapplied justification by faith simply because most first-century Jews seemed assured about their salvation. While there is truth to this (Paul is clearly confident in himself and his goodness in Phil. 3:4-6), the NPP has partially misread both the 1st century and Paul (see *Where is Boasting: Early Jewish Soteriology and Paul's Response in Romans 1-5* by Simon Gathercole). Paul's boasting and Luther's failure have the same root problem—a heart curved in on itself. Both are on the Failure-Boasting chart. Both need justification. See also John Barclay's *Paul and the Gift*. Barclay analyzes different 1st century Jewish approaches to grace showing how, yes, 1st century Judaism did have a theology of grace, but, no, it was different from Paul's. What makes Paul's grace so radical is that it is grace for the ungodly, those not worthy or deserving of grace ("incongruent grace"). See also *Paul and the Law* by Frank Thielman.

6. (Lesson 7, Sections 2 & 3) Richard Hays and N. T. Wright redefine *faith* as *faithfulness*. This view, though not technically part of the NPP discussion (Dunn disagrees with Hays and Wright), dominates among mainstream scholars, and has the effect of reinforcing the NPP focus on obedience at the expense of faith. I found Moises Silva's article in *Vol. 2, Justification and Variegated Nomism* and Kevin McFadden's article, "Does ΠΙΣΤΙΣ mean 'faith(fulness)' in Paul?," particularly helpful.

BIBLIOGRAPHY

I've made the bibliography topical so you can read some of my source material on your own. I've put an asterisk (*) next to books that I've found particularly helpful. A double asterisk (**) marks those studies I found helpful in responding to the New Perspective on Paul.

Commentaries:

Acts

Bock, Darrell L. *Acts, Baker Exegetical Commentary on the New Testament.* Grand Rapids, MI: Baker Academic, 2007.

Schnabel, Eckhard J. *Acts, Exegetical Commentary on the New Testament.* Grand Rapids, MI: Zondervan, 2012.

Wright, Tom. *Acts for Everyone, Part 2, Chapters 13-28.* Louisville, KY: Westminster John Knox Press, 2008.

Romans

**Gathercole, Simon J. *Where is Boasting? Early Jewish Soteriology and Paul's Response in Romans 1-5.* Grand Rapids, MI: Wm. B. Eerdmans Publishing Co., 2002.

Luther, Martin. "Preface to the Epistle to the Romans." *Luther's Works* 35, ed. E. Theodore Bachmann. Philadelphia: Muhlenberg, 1960.

Moo, Douglas J. *The Epistle to the Romans, The New International Commentary on the New Testament.* Grand Rapids, MI: Wm. B. Eerdmans Publishing Co., 1996.

1 and 2 Corinthians

*Clarke, Andrew D. *Secular and Christian Leadership in Corinth, A Socio-Historical and Exegetical Study of 1 Corinthians 1-6.* Eugene, OR: Wipf and Stock Publishers, 2006.

Forbes, Christopher. *Comparison, Self-Praise and Irony: Paul's Boasting and the Conventions of Hellenistic Rhetoric, New Testament Studies.* Cambridge, UK: Cambridge University Press, 1986.

Garland, David E. *1 Corinthians, Baker Exegetical Commentary on the New Testament.* Grand Rapids, MI: Baker Academic, 2003.

Garland, David E. *2 Corinthians, The New American Commentary, New International Version.* Nashville, TN: B & H Publishing Group, 1999.

*Harris, Murray J. *The Second Epistle to the Corinthians, The New International Greek Testament Commentary.* Grand Rapids, MI: Wm. B. Eerdmans Publishing Co., 2005.

*Thiselton, Anthony C. *The First Epistle to the Corinthians, The New Greek Testament Commentary.* Grand Rapids, MI: Wm. B. Eerdmans Publishing Co., 2000.

Galatians

Hays, Richard B. *The Faith of Jesus Christ: The Narrative Substructure of Galatians 3:1-4:11, Second Edition.* Grand Rapids, MI: Wm. B. Eerdmans Publishing Co., 2002.

Moo, Douglas J. *Galatians, Baker Exegetical Commentary on the New Testament.* Grand Rapids, MI: Baker Academic, 2013.

Morris, Leon. *Galatians, Paul's Charter of Christian Freedom.* Downers Grove, IL: InterVarsity Press, 1996.

Philippians

Bloomquist, L. Gregory. *The Function of Suffering in Philippians.* Sheffield, England: Sheffield Academic Press, 1993.

Bockmuehl, Markus. *The Epistle to the Philippians, Black's New Testament Commentary.* Grand Rapids, MI: Baker Academic, 1998.

Hawthorne, Gerald F. and Martin Ralph P. *Word Biblical Commentary: Philippians, Revised.* Nashville, TN: Thomas Nelson Publishers, 2004.

Hooker, Morna Dorothy. *Jesus and the Servant: The Influence of the Servant Concept of Deutero-Isaiah in the New Testament.* Eugene OR: Wipf and Stock, 1959.

O'Brien, Peter T. *The Epistle to the Philippians, The New International Greek Testament Commentary.* Grand Rapids, MI: Wm. B. Eerdmans Publishing Co., 1991.

*Silva, Moises. *Philippians, Baker Exegetical Commentary on the New Testament.* Grand Rapids, MI: Baker Academic, 2005.

Thielman, Frank. *The NIV Application Commentary: Philippians.* Grand Rapids, MI: Zondervan, 1995.

Wright, N. T. *Paul and His Letter to the Philippians.* UDEMY online course, 2015: https://www.udemy.com/paul-and-his-letter-to-the-philippians/.

Wright, N. T. *Philippians, The Lordship of Christ and the Hope of the Church.* Vancouver, BC: Regent Audio, 1990.

Philemon

Dunn, James D. G. *The Epistles to the Colossians and to Philemon, The New Internationals Greek Testament Commentary.* Grand Rapids, MI: Wm. B. Eerdmans Publishing Co., 1996.

Moo, Douglas J. *The Letters to the Colossians and to Philemon, The Pillar New Testament Commentary.* Grand Rapids, MI: Wm. B. Eerdmans Publishing Co., 2008.

Church History

*Brown, Peter. *Through the Eye of a Needle, Wealth, the Fall of Rome, and the Making of Christianity in the West, 350-550 AD.* Princeton, NJ: Princeton University Press, 2012.

Teresa, Mother. *Come Be My Light: The Private Writings of the Saint of Calcutta.* Edited and with commentary by Brian Kolodiejchuk. New York, NY: Doubleday, 2007.

Thompson, Augustine. *Francis of Assisi: A New Biography.* Ithaca, NY: Cornell University Press, 2012

Early Jewish Literature

Shanks, Hershel. *Conversations with a Bible Scholar.* Washington, D.C.: Biblical Archaeology Review ebook, 1994.

"Talmud, Tractate Shabbat 13b," quoted in Hershel Shanks, *The Dead Sea Scrolls: Discovery and Meaning*. Washington D. C.: Biblical Archaeology Review ebook, 2007.

Wise, Michael O., Abegg Jr., Martin G. and Cook, Edward M. *The Dead Sea Scrolls: A New Translation*, New York: HarperCollins, 2005.

General

Jacobs, Alan. *The Narnian*. New York: Harper Collins San Francisco, 2005.

John of Landsberg. *A Letter from Jesus Christ*. New York: Crossroad, 1981.

Johnston, Mark. *Saving God: Religion After Idolatry*. Princeton, NJ: Princeton University Press, 2009.

Keller, Timothy. *Counterfeit Gods: The Empty Promises of Money, Sex, and Power, and the Only Hope that Matters*. New York: Penguin Group, 2009.

Lewis, C.S. *Mere Christianity*. New York, NY: Macmillan Publishing Co., 1952.

Malik, Charles. *The Wonder of Being*. Waco, TX: Word Books, 1974.

J-Curve in Pauline Studies

Brondos, David A. *Paul on the Cross: Reconstructing the Apostle's Story of Redemption*. Minneapolis, MN: Fortress Press, 2006.

Evans, William B. "Raised for Our Justification: Resurrection Justification in Historical and Theological Perspective." 2010 National Meeting of the Evangelical Theological Society, Atlanta, GA. Lecture.

*Gaffin Jr., Richard B. "The Usefulness of The Cross." http://beginningwithmoses.org/bt-articles/242/the-usefulness-of-the-cross.

Gorman, Michael J. *Apostle of the Crucified Lord: A Theological Introduction to Paul & His Letters*. Grand Rapids, MI: Wm. B. Eerdmans Publishing Co., 2004.

*Gorman, Michael J. *Cruciformity: Paul's Narrative Spirituality of the Cross*. Grand Rapids, MI: Wm. B. Eerdmans Publishing Co., 2001

Hood, Jason B. *Imitating God in Christ: Recapturing a Biblical Pattern*. Downers Grove, IL: InterVarsity Press, 2013.

Horbury, William, and Brian McNeil. *Suffering and Martyrdom in the New Testament: Studies Presented to G.M. Styler by the Cambridge New Testament Seminar*. Cambridge: Cambridge University Press, 1981.

Piper, John. *Filling up the Afflictions of Christ: The Cost of Bringing the Gospel to the Nations in the Lives of William Tyndale, Adoniram Judson, and John Paton*. Wheaton, IL: Crossway, 2009.

*Stott, John R. W. *The Cross of Christ*. Downer's Grove, IL: InterVarsity Press, 1986.

*Tannehill, Robert C. *Dying and Rising with Christ: A Study in Pauline Theology*. Eugene, OR: Wipf and Stock Publishers, 2006.

Justification by Faith in Paul

Stettler, Hanna. "Did Paul Invent Justification By Faith?" *Tyndale Bulletin*, 2015.

Vickers, Brian. *Justification by Grace through Faith: Finding Freedom from Legalism, Lawlessness, Pride, and Despair*. Phillipsburg, NJ: P & R Publishing Co., 2013.

**Westerholm, Stephen. *Justification Reconsidered: Rethinking a Pauline Theme*. Grand Rapids, MI: Wm. B. Eerdmans Publishing Company, 2013.

Martin Luther and the Reformation

Clark, John C. "Martin Luther's View of Cross-Bearing." *Bibliotheca Sacra* 163, no.651 (July-September 2006).

Luther, Martin. *Galatians.* The Crossway Classic Commentaries, series ed. Alistair McGrath and J.I. Packer. Wheaton, IL: Crossway Books, 1998.

————. *Luther's Works, Volume 51.* Ed. and trans. John W. Doberstein, general ed. Helmut T. Lehmann. Philadelphia, PA: Muhlenberg Press, 1959

McGrath, Alister E. *Iustitia Dei: A History of the Christian Doctrine of Justification.* Cambridge: Cambridge University Press, 2005.

Rittgers, Ronald K. *The Reformation of Suffering: Pastoral Theology and Lay Piety in Late Medieval and Early Modern Germany.* New York, NY: Oxford Press, 2012.

Trueman, Carl. *The Reformation – 33 Lectures* (Westminster Seminary Class on iTunes).

Trueman, Carl. *Luther on the Christian Life: The Cross and Freedom.* Wheaton, IL: Crossway, 2015.

The New Perspective on Paul

**Barclay, John. *Paul and the Gift.* Grand Rapids, MI: Wm. B. Eerdmans Publishing Co., 2015.

**Gathercole, Simon. *Defending Substitution.* Grand Rapids, MI: Baker Academic, 2015.

**Irons, Charles Lee. The Righteousness of God: A Lexical Examination of the Covenant-Faithfulness Interpretation. WUNT II/386. Tübingen: Mohr Siebeck, 2015.

Justification and Variegated Nomism: Volume 1—The Complexities of Second Temple Judaism, ed. D. A. Carson, Peter T. O'Brien, Mark A. Seifrid. Grand Rapids, MI: Baker Academic, 2001.

***Justification and Variegated Nomism: Volume 2—The Paradoxes of Paul,* ed. D. A. Carson, Peter T. O'Brien, Mark A. Seifrid. Grand Rapids, MI: Baker Academic, 2004.

**Ortlund, Dane. *Zeal Without Knowledge.* New York: Bloomsbury, 2012.

Piper, John. *The Future of Justification: A Response to N.T. Wright.* Wheaton, IL: Crossway, 2007.

Wright, Nicholas Thomas. *Paul and the Faithfulness of God: Book I, Parts I and II.* Minneapolis, MN: Fortress Press, 2013.

Wright, Nicholas Thomas. *Paul and the Faithfulness of God: Parts III and IV.* London: Fortress Press, 2013.

Wright, Nicholas Thomas. *Paul: In Fresh Perspective.* Minneapolis, MN: Fortress Press, 2005.

Wright, N. T. (Nicholas Thomas.) *The Paul Debate, Critical Questions for Understanding the Apostle.* Waco, TX: Baylor University Press, 2015.

New Testament Theology

Hays, Richard B. *The Moral Vision of the New Testament: Community, Cross, New Creation: A Contemporary Introduction to New Testament Ethics.* New York, NY: HarperCollins Publishers, 1996.

Ladd, George Eldon. *A Theology of the New Testament, Revised Edition.* Grand Rapids, MI: Wm. B. Eerdmans Publishing Co., 1993.

Pauline Theology

Bruce, F. F. *Paul: Apostle of the Heart Set Free.* Grand Rapids, MI: Wm. B. Eerdmans Publishing Co.,1984.

*Gaffin, Richard B., Jr. *By Faith, Not by Sight.* Phillipsburg, NJ: P&R Publishing, 2013.

*Gaffin, Richard B., Jr. *Resurrection and Redemption.* Grand Rapids, MI: Baker Book House, 1987.

Hawthorne, Gerald F., Ralph P. Martin, Daniel G. Reid, eds. *Dictionary of Paul and His Letters: A Compendium of Contemporary Biblical Scholarship.* Downers Grove, IL: Intervarsity Press, 2015.

Kreeft, Peter. "The Twelve Most Profound Ideas I Have Ever Had." Peter Kreeft blog. http://www.peter-kreeft.com/topics-more/12-ideas.htm, accessed December 24, 2014.

Kruse, Colin G. *Paul, the Law, and Justification.* Peabody, MA: Hendrickson Publishers, Inc., 1996.

**McFadden, Kevin W. "Does ΠΙΣΤΙΣ mean 'faith(fulness)' in Paul?" *Tyndale Bulletin 66.2*, 2015.

Murray, John. *Redemption, Accomplished and Applied.* Grand Rapids, MI: Wm. B. Eerdmans Pub., 1955.

Nanos, Mark D. "Paul's Reversal of Jews Calling Gentiles 'Dogs' (Philippians 3:2),): 1600 Years of an Ideological Tale Wagging an Exegetical Dog?," *Biblical Interpretation* 17 (2009)

Ridderbos, Herman. *Paul: An Outline of His Theology.* Translated by John Richard De Witt. Grand Rapids, MI: Wm. B. Eerdmans Publishing Co., 1975.

**Schreiner, Thomas R. "Works of Law in Paul." *Novum Testamentum* XXXIII, 3, 1991.

Thielman, Frank. *Paul and the Law: A Contextual Approach.* Downers Grove, IL: InterVarsity Press, 1994.

*Vos, Geerhardus. *Pauline Eschatology.* Phillipsburg, NJ: P & R Publishing Co., 1979.

Union with Christ in Pauline Theology

Campbell, Constantine R. *Paul and Union with Christ: An Exegetical and Theological Study.* Grand Rapids, MI: Zondervan, 2012.

*Evans, William. *Imputation and Impartation: Union with Christ in American Reformed Theology.* Eugene, OR: Wipf and Stock Publishers, 2008.

Fitzpatrick, Elyse M. *Found in Him: The Joy of the Incarnation and Our Union with Christ.* Wheaton, IL: Crossway, 2013.

Wilbourne, Rankin, *Union with Christ.* Colorado Springs, CO: David C. Cook, 2016.

About

seeJesus is a global discipling mission passionate about equipping the worldwide church to reflect all the beauty of Jesus. We invite you to learn more about our books, Bible studies, and seminars:

 Subscribe at info@seejesus.net

 @_PaulEMiller

 Facebook/seeJesus.net

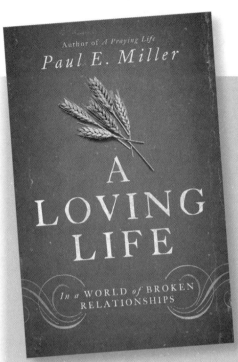

UNCOVER THE TRUTH ABOUT LOVE

A Loving Life tackles the age old questions at the heart of our struggle to love. Drawing on the book of Ruth, Miller helps us embrace relationship, endure rejection, cultivate community, and reach out to even the most unlovable around us as we discover the power to love.

"Every once in a great while one reads a book that is so profound, so fresh, and so life changing that you can't get it out of your mind or your heart. A Loving Life is that kind of book."

Steve Brown, host, Key Life radio program

DISCOVER THE JOY OF REAL PRAYER

Paul Miller's best-selling book, now in its second edition, invites us to ask God for help with the nitty-gritty details of life. Pray through everything from parking spots to contact lenses and discover the freedom and joy of a vibrant prayer life. Discussion guide now available.

"A great book on prayer—biblical, practical, readable. This book will help you generate a culture of prayer in you and those around you."

Tim Keller, senior pastor, Redeemer Presbyterian Church and author of *The Reason for God*

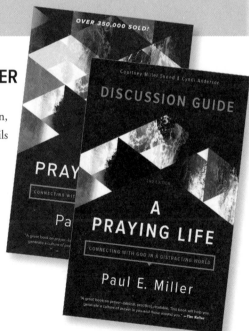

Available at **seeJesus.net**

JOIN JESUS ON THE J-CURVE

Jesus' life had a shape—a repeated pattern of dying and rising we call the "J-Curve." Explore the J-Curve through the writings of the apostle Paul in this series of six interactive Bible studies from Paul Miller. Find renewed hope and deeper fellowship with God's people as you walk out Jesus' pattern of dying and rising in your everyday life.

"Take time with the J-Curve. You will become a deeper, wiser, truer person. You will become more humble, more joyous, more purposeful. And you will walk more steadily in the Light."

David Powlison, Director of CCEF

WATCH JESUS BRING GRACE TO LIFE

Explore the gospel of Luke through this 18-lesson interactive Bible study and discover a richly textured world filled with the beauty of God's character and the transformative truth about grace.

"This is no mere fill-in-the-blank Bible study. It's more like a fill-in-the-heart exploration of the only love that is better than life."

Scotty Smith, West End Community Church (Nashville, TN)